WAL[...] THE WHIT[...] COUNTRY

Fifteen Country Rambles near Oxford, Swindon and Newbury

NIGEL HAMMOND

with Historical Notes

COUNTRYSIDE BOOKS
NEWBURY, BERKSHIRE

First Published 1982
© Nigel Hammond 1982

COUNTRYSIDE BOOKS
3 Catherine Road
Newbury, Berkshire

ISBN 0 905392 14 0

Thanks are due to Peter Bradley, Deputy Editor,
Abingdon Herald Series of Newspapers, and to
Oxford County Newspapers for permission to use
material in this book which originally appeared in a
series of 'Afoot' articles in their columns.

Thanks are also due to Oxfordshire County Council
for providing the cover photograph of the Ridgeway.

Designed by Mon Mohan
Maps drawn by David Thelwell
Printed in England by J.W. Arrowsmith Ltd., Bristol
Typeset by Datchet Printing Services, Datchet, Berkshire

Contents

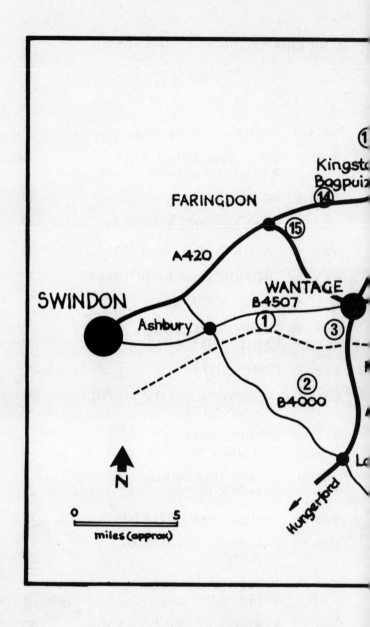

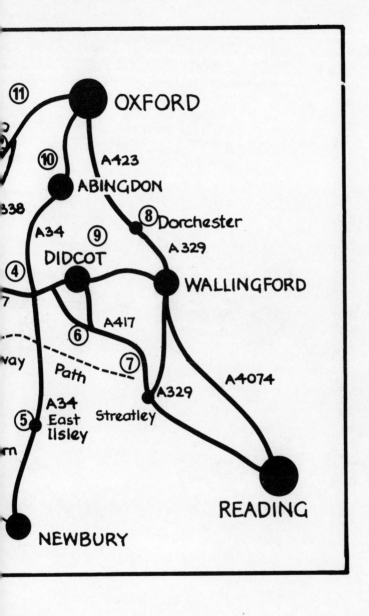

Publisher's Introduction

The routes in this book have been carefully chosen to take advantage of the variety of scenery which there is for the walker throughout the area of the Vale of the White Horse. There are short walks, long walks, breezy walks on top of the downs, and quiet strolls by the riverside.

All of them are circular and most can be completed in a few hours. On some there is the option of a shorter route in addition to the main one. For those who like to stop for refreshment the names of good pubs along the way are mentioned; but where there is no pub there is usually a suitable spot for a picnic. Historical Notes, providing basic information about the many places of interest on each walk, are in a section that immediately follows the text of the route itself.

The sketch maps are designed to guide walkers to the starting point and give a simple overall idea of the route to be taken. For those who like the benefit of detailed maps the relevant Ordnance Survey 1:50,000 series sheet is recommended; either no. 164 or 174.

The walks are all along public footpaths and highways, but bear in mind that deviation orders may be made from time to time. Please also remember the Country Code and make sure gates are not left open nor any farm animals disturbed.

Finally, a stout pair of shoes is recommended for all the walks. Even on the driest summer day there will usually be at least one muddy patch.

Nicholas Battle

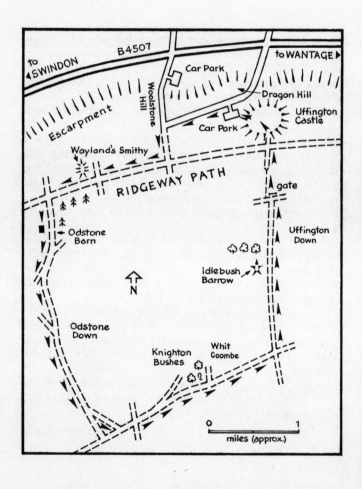

White Horse Hill and Wayland's Smithy

Introduction: This walk circuits one of the most historic and mystical areas associated with the Vale of the White Horse. It takes in White Horse Hill and Uffington Castle, while Dragon's Hill is not far away, and Wayland's Smithy is on the course. All of these sites of antiquity are deeply related to the region's history, and steeped in legend and tradition.

The walk itself affords a pleasant upland variation from the flat and wooded Vale. You walk from the National Trust area of White Horse Hill to Wayland's Smithy. Another National Trust property is close at hand, namely Ashdown House just to the west, as are the Blowingstone at the foot of Kingstone Lisle Hill, and Seven Barrows out towards Lambourn.

You can quite easily deviate from the circuit if you feel so inclined, as the whole area is criss-crossed by paths, tracks and bridleways, and the area offers the walker the ability to roam a safe network of paths.

Distance: The walk's route is about $6^1/_2$ miles long and should take some 3-4 hours to complete, although longer depending upon how much time you spend at the historic sites nearby.

Refreshments: White Horse Hill is a marvellous site for picnics, and in summer months there is sometimes an ice-cream vendor in the area. However, as you pass no inns and go through no villages, it might be as well to take your own refreshments with you.

How to get there: By car using the B4507 from Swindon or Wantage, or by minor roads through Uffington from

Stanford-in-the-Vale on the A417 from Faringdon to Wantage. The way up to White Horse Hill is clearly signposted and a one-way system is in operation. At the summit a car park for the disabled and elderly is adjacent to the hill itself, while further along and to the right is another extensive car park.

The Walk: From the car park for the disabled and elderly at the summit of the hill walk along the exit road until you reach the road running up Woolstone HIll. There you turn left and walk for 400 yards to the Ridgeway, where you turn right along the track. From the main car park, join the route by simply walking straight up Woolstone Hill.

In 500 yards you come to Wayland Smith's Cave, a chambered long-barrow, which can be reached through a field gate on the right. The site was immortalised by Sir Walter Scott in Kenilworth who came to know this area through the Hughes family of Uffington.

The legend of Wayland the Smith as told by Scott is a fair summary. It runs thus: "You must tie your horse to that stone which has a ring in it, you must whistle three times, put your money on the flat stone, sit down for ten minutes. You will hear a hammer clink. Then say your prayers, and you will find your money gone and the horse shod." See also the historical notes.

After visiting the cave, walk a further 300 yards along the Ridgeway to a crossing of tracks and turn left along a wide and dusty track which passes (for the time being) through sheltered belts of conifers. On your right you pass Odstone Barn, a black painted corrugated building. The track gently descends between hawthorn hedges then, equally gently, begins to rise again to a prominent clump of beech trees on the left of the track.

Another shelter belt crosses the track, which then bends to the right and continues a gentle rise over open fields with extensive views to both left and right. The track continues up the side of Odstone Down and near the top bears left.

There is a wood just visible over the curve about 100 yards to the right, and soon another track joins from the right.

The track now begins a gentle descent and Maddle Farm emerges into view half left. In due course an obvious track branches over rough grass to the left and descends quite steeply. You take this route and at the foot of the hill join a track from the right.

You are now walking about due east with pasture fields extending to Maddle Farm on the right. The number of small hawthorns beside the track increases hereabouts and a track joins the route from the right, but the walk continues ahead and curves to the left to the corner of a beech wood in an area known as Knighton Bushes.

Turn right along the right-hand side of the wood, which is with you for several hundred yards. At the end of the wood the track winds a little, then begins a long but gentle haul up the side of Whit Coombe. In almost ¾ mile you reach the summit and your advance is barred by a wooden fence and racehorse gallop. Turn left, following the small footpath sign over soft grass on the left of the gallop. You will be gently ascending.

Looking half right there is a good view over the downland with Kingston Warren Farm and Hill Barn Clump in a straight line, and due right you will see the radio mast at Sparsholt Firs on the skyline.

In due course you will come to a Clapham Junction of gallops where you bear left, following the small path sign, heading for what looks like a pimple on the skyline, but which is Idlebush barrow, which you pass on the left.

Uffington Castle on the summit of White Horse Hill is now on the skyline, and beyond Idlebush Barrow you pass off the gallops through a shelter belt of young beech trees on to a well-defined track which runs ahead.

At the end of the track you pass through a metal field gate and immediately turn left then right around the field boundary. It is now an easy walk back to the Ridgeway some 700 yards ahead, which you cross and enter the back of Uffington Castle, turning left around the SW sector of the enclosing rampart which you follow until you reach the western exit.

Turn left and walk down the steep slope to the car park, where the walk began.

Historical Notes:

White Horse Hill is the focal point of the Vale and the Berkshire Downs, and is an area of pilgrimage from far and near. As part of the chalk upland, it rises some 856 feet above sea level and is one of the highest points. At the top of the hill, Uffington Castle forms an Iron Age Hill Fort some 82 acres in extent. Of spade-head shape it has a single entrance on the west and was probably built at the time of the second Iron Age immigration about 350BC as a defensive site against later invaders. It was the site of numerous feasts and revels in the 18th and 19th centuries when local people came here to let their hair down and to complete the periodic "scourings" of the White Horse. Such a Scouring, or cleaning, was held in 1857, and the handbill advertising the Revel ran as follows:

PASTIME

To be held on the occasion of the Scouring of the White Horse, September 17th and 18th, 1857.

At a meeting held at the Craven Arms, Uffington, on the 20th day of August 1857, the following resolutions were passed unanimously:-

First: That a pastime be held on the White Horse Hill, on Thursday and Friday, the 17th and 18th of September, in accordance with the old custom at the time of "The Scouring of the Horse".

2dly: That E. Martin Atkins, Esq. of Kingston Lisle, be appointed Treasurer.

3dly: That prizes be awarded for the following game and sports.

That is to say –

Backsword	*Old gamesters*	*£8*
Play	*Young gamesters*	*£4*
Wrestling	*Old gamesters*	*£5*
	Young gamesters	*£4*

A Jingling match
Foot races
Hurdle races
Race of cart-horses in Thill harness (for a new set of harness)
Donkey race (for a flitch of bacon)
Climbing pole (for a leg of mutton)
Races down the Manger (for cheeses)

A pig will be turned out on the down, to be the prize of the man who catches him (under certain regulations); and further prizes will be awarded for other games and sports as the funds will allow.

4thly: That no person be allowed to put up or use a stall or booth on the ground, without the previous sanction of Mr. Spackman, of Bridgecombe Farm (the occupier), who is hereby authorized to make terms with any person wishing to put up a stall or booth.

Signed. E. MARTIN ATKINS, Chairman.

In addition, well-known was the dialect ballad of the Scouring of the White Horse:

The owld White Horse wants zettin to rights,
 And the Squire hev promised good cheer,
Zo we'll gee un a scrape to kip 'un in zhape,
 And a'll last for many a year.

A was made a lang lang time ago
 Wi a good dale o' labour and pains,
By King Alfred the Great when he spwiled their consate
 And caddled they wosbirds the Danes.

The Bleawien Stwun in days gone by
 Wur King Alfred's bugle harn,
And the tharnin tree you may plainly see
 As is called King Alfred's tharn.

There'll be backsword play, and climmin the powl,
 And a race for a peg, and a cheese,
And us thenks as hisn's a dummel zowl
 As dwont care for zich spwoorts as theze.

The White Horse's origin is shrouded in the mists of the past. Was it perhaps cut to commemorate Alfred's great victory in 871 over the Danes at the Battle of Ashdown, or maybe cut as a tribal emblem of the Dobunni? It might even be a thousand years older than this, but certainly it resembles a stylised horse which has been found on Iron Age pottery and may therefore come from the period 100BC-100AD.

Dragon's Hill, though, may be artificial. Soil tests show a high potach content, some double the average of the area at its summit. Could it have been a beacon site, or a site for Sacrifices to be offered? Alternatively some say it may have been raised to give added height to direct the accurate cutting of the White Horse. A kind of podium in front of the hill.

Wayland's Smithy, on the other hand, lying some 50 yards from the Ridgeway is a ruined Neolithic burial site, the largest stone of which remains in situ, resting on five others. The remaining stones lie scattered about. The whole formed a sepulchural chamber and was originally covered with earth and chalk. The date of construction is put at between 3,500BC and 3,000BC.

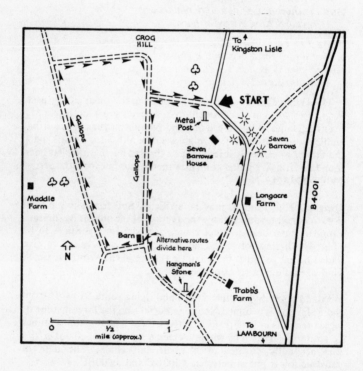

CROG HILL

To Kingston Lisle

START

Gallops

Metal Post

Seven Barrows

Seven Barrows House

Gallops

Maddle Farm

Longacre Farm

N

Barn

Alternative routes divide here

Hangman's Stone

Trabb's Farm

B4001

To LAMBOURN

0   ½   1
mile (approx.)

Seven Barrows

Introduction: A day on the Downs can be a pleasure whatever the season of the year particularly if you walk regularly and do not mind the winter cold and wind. But really this walk near Seven Barrows to the north of Lambourn is most enjoyable during the warmer months, particularly as it is completely in open countryside, passing through no village, but occasionally skirting a farm or house sheltering in one of the valleys close to the access roads. The walk passes three items of interest, namely the hangman's stone, the metal boundary post close to the start, and the important series of late Neolithic Bronze Age barrows known as Seven Barrows, although if you cound them carefully, you will find that there are certainly more than seven. Go prepared for changes in weather, for the course of the walks is open and windswept, although the tracks and paths are likely to remain dry except after exceptionally heavy rain.

Distance: You can get two basic walks out of this figure of eight of footpaths and bridleways. The two basic walks are each just over $3^1/_2$ miles long and begin from the northern end of Seven Barrows near Westcot Down (MR324833) where there is some suitable parking beside and just off the road. Both walks have a common route for $1^1/_2$ miles then divide.

Refreshments: If you wish to find an inn and some food you should call at nearby Lambourn; there are no refreshments near the route, but the whole area provides a large number of extremely good picnic sites particularly close to the two small areas of woodland, near metal post and Maddle Farm.

How to get there: From Lambourn take the Wantage road and bear left after $1\frac{1}{2}$ miles towards Kingston Lisle, or from the Wantage to Swindon road (B4507) turn south at Kingston Lisle cross road and pass up the steep Blowingstone Hill. You come to the start of the walk in about two miles, indicated by a waist-high iron post at the side of the road marking the county boundary.

The Walk: You set off from the metal post beside the road, which also marks the boundary of Kingston Lisle and Lambourn parish, across the level track over Westcot Down. After 300 yards you pass beside a substantial beech wood at the far end of which is the discernible outline of a long barrow on the right.

Keep straight on for a further 400 yards where at a T-junction of bridle tracks you turn left beside a race-horse gallop. At first the track is grassy and level, then turns into a flinty track and rises gently to Post Down, where it levels out again on the summit.

In due course the open downland track turns into a damp and shady lane running between hawthorns and oaks. Some 500 yards from the summit of Post Down you come to a Dutch barn and track junction on the right. This is where the walks divide.

The main walk continues ahead and bends slightly to the left along the very well-defined lane. Some 700 yards from the barn you come to Hangman's Stone on the left, a sarsen stone some four feet in height, planted on the side of the track. Walk a further 100 yards then turn very sharp left on to another track, which is at first level, then leads by way of a shelter belt down the side of Wether Down. Continue along this track, which levels out near Trabb's Farm, then undulates until it joins the Lambourn road at Longacre Farm.

Take the road ahead which runs straight for 500 yards then swings left through the centre of the Seven Barrows. You pass Sevenbarrows House on the left, a substantial race-horse stables and in some 300 yards the walk ends at the metal post.

If you choose to do the second walk it continues from the Dutch barn, where you turn right along a metalled road giving access to the gallops. In a short step the road turns left and the walk bears right onto a track to the left of the gallops.

Some 600 yards on, a wood runs down on the left, Baldback Covert by name, to Maddle Farm in the hollow below. From here the track undulates and gradually rises up the back of the chalk. At the end of the gallop on the right, you turn right on to a well-defined track.

It is a long descent with good views ahead and to the left over the surrounding countryside. At Crog Hill the track quickly swings round to the right and in a couple of hundred yards you turn left on to the track which you used from the metal post to Westcot Down wood. It is about 600 yards to the metal post where the walk began.

You can add to these two walks by doing the outside circuit of them each of which is about 4$^1/_2$ miles in length, or by doing a figure of eight.

Historical Notes:

Seven Barrows. If you should care to count them you will find many more than seven. There were originally some forty in all; twenty of them are still quite clearly distinguishable, but others, over the last couple of centuries, have been ploughed virtually out of existence. Most of those visible today are Round Barrows and come from the Bronze Age. Many have been excavated and finds include the remains of a bronze awl, various ornamental daggers and an incense cup. One chambered Long Barrow close by was discovered as recently as 1935. It is surprising that a barrow some 220 feet long and about 50 feet across should have remained undiscovered until then. It was found by the author of *The Ancient Burial Mounds of England,* Mr E.V. Grinsell, who was apparently taking a walk in this area. The barrow, though, had one end ploughed out, while a grass bank ran across the other end which together with a cart track caused the sarsen stones which originally formed the passage and chambers of the barrow to become exposed. Mr Grinsell, who was an expert in these matters pieced the riddle together and found the missing barrow.

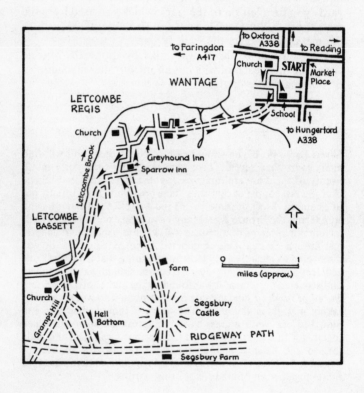

Wantage and Segsbury Castle

Introduction:

> Alfred found learning dead and he restored it,
> Education neglected and he revived it,
> The laws powerless and he gave them force,
> The church debased and he raised it,
> The land ravaged by a fearful enemy
> From which he delivered it.
> Alfred's name will live as long
> As mankind shall respect the past.

The walk begins at King Alfred's statue in the picturesque market place of Wantage, his birthplace. It takes you beside the weed-waving Letcombe Brook, through the picture post-card Letcombe villages, to the open windswept Ridgeway. You may have to pause for breath just south of Letcombe Bassett, but the steep climb to the summit is worth the superb view over Devil's Punchbowl. The walk also passes through the impressive Iron Age Fort called Segsbury Castle, sited ominously on the edge of the Downs overlooking the whole of the White Horse Vale.

Distance: The route chosen is about six miles long. It is for the most part easy going and should take 3-4 hours to complete. If you wish, the walk may be shortened by starting at Letcombe Regis.

Refreshments: There are ample inns and several cafes in Wantage, while you pass the Greyhound and the Sparrow Inns in Letcombe Regis. The countryside on the Downs above the village is ideal for picnics.

How to get there: By car, Wantage is easily reached from the surrounding towns and villages with direct roads from the Oxford, Reading, Newbury and Faringdon areas. There is parking in the market place and in the several car parks hidden behind the main square.

The Walk: From the Market Place, pass through Wantage churchyard and turn along Priory Road. Cross the main road at King Alfred's School, walk to the right for a few yards, then follow the narrow lane which leads off the road to the left. It crosses allotments then plunges into farmland beside the Letcombe Brook. In under a mile the pathway will see you on the edge of Letcombe Regis.

At the first crossroad, walk ahead and, passing the Greyhound Inn, follow the metalled road to the church. Here you turn left and begin to walk slightly uphill between high manorial walls on one side and a raised footpath on the other. You pass a wide variety of village houses and cottages. Follow the road quickly right and left and left again.

At this point, where spectacular views of the Downland escarpment open up, take the track to the right. If you need it, a metal seat offers the opportunity of rest and contemplation of the fine view, while a hundred yards away to the left is the Sparrow Inn, which can offer rest and good refreshment.

You have sheltered parkland on the right, and open ploughland, rising at first gently, to the hills, on the left. Pass along the track and after 200 yards turn left. In another 100 yards take a narrow footpath to the right. You will cross pasture, then walk at the edge of a deep valley above the Letcombe Brook. This is a sheltered footpath, and the high hedgerow hides a landscape a whole world apart from the bleak openness of the Downland.

Very soon you join the road entering Letcombe Bassett at White's Farm. Passing a racehorse stable on the left, you come to a junction near the village centre. You turn left here, but if for a moment you walk ahead, you will quickly realise why Thomas Hardy called this settlement "Cresscombe" in "Jude the Obscure." The site of Letcombe watercress beds lies to the left around the springs from which the chalk stream rises. Isolated on the water's edge, the small cottage, called Arabella's Cottage, is by repute where Jude, having

20

walked over the Downs from Marygreen (Fawley) came across Arabella washing pig's chitterlings in the stream.

Return to the junction by the village shop and walk uphill. The church lies a few steps to the right, but walk ahead following the road uphill along the route which Hardy has Jude using from Fawley.

There are now three possible ways to reach the Ridgeway. The first is to take the indicated footpath to the left just where the road curves right. This footpath passes across fields, through Hell Bottom, and then ascends very sharply to the Ridgeway.

If this is not your choice, follow the road a little further to the fork and take the left branch up to Parsonage Hill and the Ridgeway.

The third choice is to continue ahead up Gramp's Hill. A splendid panorama will unfold to the right, not only into the chasm of Devil's Punchbowl, but right over the Vale of the White Horse to Faringdon and beyond.

Whichever path you use to the Ridgeway, when you get there turn left along this ancient green road, used from time immemorial as a major routeway and drove road across southern England, linking London markets with animal raising and fattening grounds in Wales and the west.

The Ridgeway undulates over Parsonage Hill and Rat's Hill, where the alternative paths from Letcombe join the walk. From Rat's Hill you walk for about 900 yards to Segsbury Farm, which lies in shelter away from the Ridgeway to the right.

Almost opposite the farm, take a track to the left which passes through the centre of Segsbury Castle (see the historical notes). It is an interesting detour to walk round the rampart, but if you do, it will add almost a mile to the total distance.

Follow the track down Castle Hill. It has become a metalled road, and in the centre of the plain formed by the lower chalk, you pass Warborough Farm and cottages.

Near the foot of the hill isolated houses and cottages lie away from the road to the right and very quickly you pass into Letcombe Regis. Turn left at the Sparrow Inn, then follow the road through the village. Take the footpath across the fields back to the Market Place at Wantage where the walk began.

Historical Notes:

Wantage, one of the main market towns in the Vale of the White Horse, is famous as the birth place of King Alfred in 849. The marble statue of the king was carved by Count Gleichen and presented to the town by Lord Wantage in 1877, with, it is said, a facial likeness of the Noble Lord!

Take a look at the blue and red brick buildings on the southern side of the market. They are excellent examples of the regional building style of the 18th century. The church, at the western end of the market, dates from the late 13th century and was restored by the distinguished local architect George Street, in 1857. It holds a fine monument in the chancel to Sir William Fitzwarin (1361) and a brass to Sir Ivo Fitzwarin (1414), reputedly both of the family from the Dick Whittington story.

In Priory Road you pass part of the Victorian former Convent buildings of the Wantage Order, namely the old Retreat House of St Michael's, while on the left at Portway is King Alfred's School, formerly an ancient Grammar School but rebuilt on this site in 1850.

Letcombe Regis is a typical spring-line (i.e. one situated close to the division of the underlying clay and chalk strata) village composed of picturesque thatched cottages and more substantial village houses. St Andrew's church has a 13th century tower, a Norman font, and some original early stained glass.

Letcombe Bassett is the source of the Letcombe Brook below which, in a deeply incised ravine, are the watercress beds which once made the village well-known. Arabella's Cottage comes straight from Thomas Hardy's Jude the Obscure. St Michael's Church possesses a Norman Chancel, but the rest of the building was largely restored in 1861 by William Butterfield.

Segsbury Castle, the Iron Age Hill Fort just north of the Ridgeway, is enclosed all round by a single ditch and rampart, with the original entrance probably facing east. The Camp encloses a total of $26\frac{1}{4}$ acres and the ramparts were originally faced with massive sarsen stones taken from the underlying chalk. Virtually all of these have been removed over the centuries and used as local building stone. Several Iron Age pottery finds have been unearthed within the camp, and a Saxon burial site came to light in the 19th century on the southern portion of the rampart.

East Hendred and Steventon

Introduction: This is a walk which can quite easily be started from either end. If you come from the Abingdon direction, you can begin at Steventon Green, but if you come from Wantage, Newbury or Didcot, the most convenient start point is in East Hendred. This is the starting point for the route described here. The walk itself takes you through easy but interestingly undulating countryside near the eastern end of the Vale of the White Horse.

Steventon and East Hendred are two of the most delightful villages in the district. The former boasts a substantial collection of pretty timbered, plaster and brick houses edging the raised and flagged Causeway, many of them having plaster patterns on their frontages in East Anglian style. East Hendred, on the other hand, has well-spaced, substantial manor and village houses, interspersed with quaint cottages, as befits a village once having important market functions with a well-known woollen manufacturing trade. Today, its functions are more related to people working at neighbouring Harwell and other employment centres in the region, although the village has a race-horse establishment and a substantial proportion of retired people.

Distance: The full circuit (including Steventon) is about $5\frac{1}{2}$ miles in length, and although the time taken for a walk varies so much with the individual and the conditions of the day, it took me almost three hours to complete.

Refreshments: You may choose to call in at the Eyston

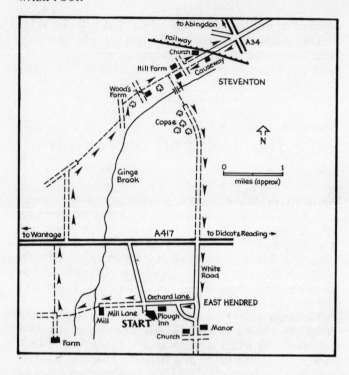

Arms or the Plough Inn at East Hendred, which village also has a couple of general stores, or alternatively there is the North Star Inn along the Causeway in Steventon.

How to get there: From Abingdon take the road south over the river Ock bridge through Drayton and Steventon. From Wantage take the A417 going east towards Rowstock and Didcot; turn right into East Hendred after 2¹/₂ miles.

The Walk: When you reach East Hendred, park near the Plough Inn, where you can get a good ploughman's lunch. From the inn turn left and walk west along Orchard Lane, going over the crossroads and down Mill Lane. You pass houses on the right and a playing field on the left, then gently descend to the mill, which lies on the Ginge Brook.

Take the gate to the right of the mill and walk across the field ahead, slightly to the left, taking an obvious footbridge over a tributary stream. The path takes you on to a field boundary where you cross a stile and follow the hedgerow on your left. In a few hundred yards you will come to a track leading down to a farm on the left. Turn right and follow the boundary for some 300 yards to the Wantage-Rowstock road, which you should cross with care.

The footpath leads directly from the other side of the road as a farm track. In a couple of hundred yards you come to a slightly submerged footpath between two hedges. Turn right along the outside hedgerow for a further two hundred yards. You pass through a hedgerow into a ploughed field over which the farmer has left unploughed a narrow pathway. In a hundred yards it joins a track at right angles. Turn left and follow the track, which degenerates into a path, to Wood's Farm.

The footpath follows the side of an orchard for a few hundred yards then, well defined, crosses into a pasture. Keep the Ginge Brook quite close to your right and you will not go far wrong. You follow this path for about 500 yards, then turn right over a footbridge.

In order to visit Steventon, however, keep ahead on the clear footpath. Pass through Hill Farm after about 400 yards and, when you join a metalled road, continue ahead. You will soon come onto the Causeway which leads you quickly into Steventon. Rejoin the walk at the footbridge by returning along the same route.

From the footbridge walk up the gently rising path that runs along the field boundary. In 400 yards the path turns into a track which you follow for almost a mile to the Wantage-Rowstock road on the edge of East Hendred. Cross the road into White Road, and in 300 yards turn right into Orchard Lane to regain the Plough Inn where the walk began.

Historical Notes:

East Hendred: This is one of the prettiest of the medium-sized villages at the edge of the Downs. In the Middle Ages it was famous for its cloth industry, and an important annual fair was held on the Golden Mile, a green road stretching from the village to the Ridgeway at Scutchamore Knob. The former prosperity of Hendred is attested to by the large number of fine timber-built houses, some thatched, others gabled.

Champ's Chapel. Close to the village entrance, was built by the Carthusian Monks of Shene in Surrey who were former owners of one of Hendred's Manors.

The Manor. It belongs to the Eyston family whose ancestors acquired the manor by marriage in 1450. They were connected by marriage with Sir Thomas More, of whom there is a picture in the house. The Roman Catholic Chapel attached to the house is one of the very few in England in which services have been continuously held. It was plundered by the soldiers of William of Orange when they passed through Hendred. They dressed up a "Mawkin" in the chapel vestments, then burned it on a bonfire in a street at Oxford.

The Church dates from 1200 and among several interesting features are the Eyston Chapel of 1500, the clock dating from 1528 and one of the oldest in England still working, while a handsome Jacobean pulpit has a sounding board and a clear carved head of King Charles I. There is also an overlarge egg-timer to measure the parson's sermon, and close by is a reading desk in the shape of a Crusader's foot.

Steventon: this large and picturesque village lies at the edge of the Vale of the White Horse. It is today somewhat misaligned, for the main road running through the village green, formerly the Southampton road to the Midlands and North, before the A34 bypass was built, is not the historical axis of the village.

This axis runs along the raised and flagged Causeway route through the village, running from Milton, along the southern edge of the extensive village green; a route which led into the Downs at East Hendred. At the south-western end of the Causeway was formerly a small Priory belonging to Bec Abbey. Bec held the Manor but sold the Priory late in Edward III's reign.

Along the Causeway are some six outstanding timber houses. The Priory next to the church, for instance, shows a fine set of gable ends with Oriel window and dates from 1657. Others have good barge boards and wooden mullions.

The Downs at East Ilsley

Introduction:

> 'Ilsley, remote amid the Berkshire Downs
> Claims these distinctions o'er her sister towns;
> Far famed for sheep and wool, tho' not for spinners.
> For sportsmen, doctors, publicans, and sinners.'

. . . and East Ilsley does indeed lie remote and in a cupshaped hollow of the bare, chalk, Berkshire Downs to the south of the historic Ridgeway path. It is possible to walk hereabouts without meeting another living soul and to recapture some flavour of the area when this was the centre of a great sheep rearing area and East Ilsley itself was a town thriving on regular sheep and wool markets and fairs. The walk takes in some fine Downland scenery, here open and windswept; there, enclosed, steep and deeply wooded. The circuit is suitable for any time of the year, although it is exposed in places, while in the wooded areas in wet weather it can become very muddy, so that suitable clothing may be required.

Distance: The walk is about five miles long and should take $2\frac{1}{2}$-3 hours to complete.

Refreshments: There are no pubs on the actual route of the walk, but there are some excellent ones in East Ilsley. It is quite possible to park near the church, on the south of the village close to the start of the walk.

How to get there: Take the A34 Newbury-Oxford road. The turn to East Ilsley is easily identified and clearly signposted

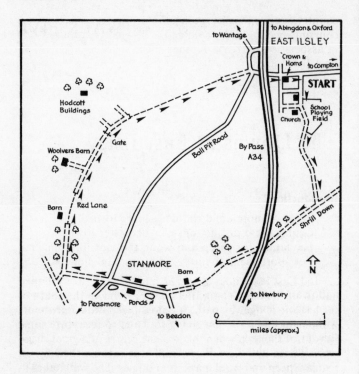

from the dual carriageway of the Ilsley by-pass. The start may also be reached along minor roads from Hampstead Norris in the east by way of Compton, and from Wantage in the west, along the B4479 then turning off through Farnborough and West Ilsley.

The Walk: From the church follow Churchside out of the village. Where the road turns right at the school, follow the rough track ahead, which leads round the right of the playing field.

The initial section of the walk is undulating and straightforward. In half a mile you steeply ascend Shrill Down. At a crossing of tracks on the top, turn right along a green road called Dennisford Road. Sheltered by regular hawthorns, the track now runs gently downhill. This is hare

28

country, and on many occasions in the last century hare coursing meetings were held on the downs hereabouts, often in association with the famous sheep markets and fairs in East Ilsley itself.

Cross the bypass carefully. The flint and pebble surfaced bridleway opposite is easy to follow, and it is a relief to get away from the roar of the traffic thundering to the docks or coastal resorts.

After 400 yards the track bears left and narrows, but is conveniently sheltered on the right by a strip of woodland. Pheasants and partridges abound on this part of the walk, for the surrounding verges and woodland provide good nesting cover.

Leaving Beedon woodland behind to the right, a good view of Beedon village and church opens up ahead, while on the horizon are the characteristic "humps" of Beacon Hill on the Hampshire Downs beyond Newbury. Bearing right at an isolated farm building, the track descends over some 500 yards to a road which runs from Beedon to Stanmore. Take a look at the good example of a roadside pond opposite, and turn right along the road. You soon pass into Stanmore, with south and north Stanmore Farms standing sentry over this largely agricultural hamlet.

At the telephone kiosk follow the unmarked bridleway to the right in the angle made by roads to Peasemore and East Ilsley. After 800 yards, at a T-junction, turn right along a holly enclosed lane. In a few yards deep woodland joins the track on the left. At Red Lane Barn, farm buildings and cottages border the track, and if there is any doubt as to why the lane is so called, you will find that following wet weather it becomes a sticky, red, muddy, mess. Beyond the buildings the track passes through a hollow, but it is very overgrown, and the footpath has diverted to run on the left above the hollow.

Onwards from here one is walking down an idyllic dry valley. The L-shape of Woolvers Barn lies to the left, and Hodcott Buildings, backed by woodland, is on the skyline. Crossing a gate at the end of the field, some 900 yards from Woolvers Barn, a bridleway joins from the left and a footpath is signposted to the right. Ignore both and walk ahead for a short distance. Where the lane turns sharply left, continue ahead along a narrow footpath which curves to the right, round the side of Windmill Hill.

In due course the path widens into a track and then joins a road which leads into East Ilsley. Pass through the bridge to the Crown & Horns. If it happens to be the right time of day, you may find this an interesting inn. As a free house it specialises in real ale including draught beers from Devenish, Fullers, Morland, Arkells and Wadworths breweries. Perhaps an apt reminder that the Morland family started their brewery here in East Ilsley!

You can return to your car by way of the hill which is the main street. The sheep markets here were said to be the largest held outside London, while the great sheep fair in August often saw over 30,000 animals up for sale. It is little wonder that Ilsley still has so many inns, for they were in large demand to quench the thirts of drovers and merchants who used the place last century.

Historical Notes:

The position of East Ilsley made it one of southern England's major sheep markets at the centre of an extensive grazing country. All that has changed. The inns that watered and fed the shepherds and drovers remain, along with one or two substantial houses once belonging to Ilsley merchants, but the permanent extensive sheep-pens, where, in the mid-18th century up to 80,000 animals were collected, have gone, together with the sheep fair and regular sheep markets of yesteryear. To some extent race-horse training and arable farming have replaced the sheep.

Kate's Gore, at the foot of Gore Hill, north of the village, is the site of one of the earliest racing establishments which belonged to George II's brother, the Duke of Cumberland, at which the celebrated horse 'Eclipse' was born in 1764. The horse won the Ascot Plate (forerunner of the Gold Cup) in 1769, and it was the Duke of Cumberland's influence which infused new life into the Ascot race meetings.

Two merchant houses, East Ilsley Hall, an early Georgian building, and Kennet House, nearly opposite and dating from about 1700, are worth examination, together with the church, some of which dates from the 12th century.

Blewburton Hill

Introduction: Beginning at Upton, this walk passes along the
Berkshire Downs by way of Churn Range and Blewbury
Down to the Ridgeway. It then passes through the narrow
defile of Hogtrough Bottom to Aston Upthorpe, and back to
Upton passing the important hill fort of Blewburton Hill and
through the picturesque village of Blewbury. Here I have
suggested rather a long walk of some 9½ miles but by using
numerous of the tracks running down from the Blewbury
Downs, it can be shortened at will. It is perhaps most
suitable as an all-day affair, exploring Lowbury Hill and
Blewburton Hill, with splendid views to take in, and with
enjoyable walking over soft downland turf.

In general the countryside is varied; the walking easy; the
gradients gentle. For the most part the going is dry, but with
a few exceptionally muddy parts — so go prepared for them,
and for the changes of weather you might expect during a 9½
mile walk in the English climate. Quite obviously, the time
taken for this walk will very much depend on the day and
upon the preferences of the individual or group, but as a
broad indication, and with several stops en route, I have
completed this circuit on my own in about four hours of fast
walking.

Refreshments: At the outset, there is an inn on the main road
at Upton, but (unless you are taking a picnic with you) there
are three good inns at Blewbury: the Blueberry Inn and the
Barley Mow together with the Load of Mischief. There is
also a tea room in a house just off the main A417 where it
passes through the village; this is some four-fifths around the
walk, and an afternoon tea might be most welcome.

31

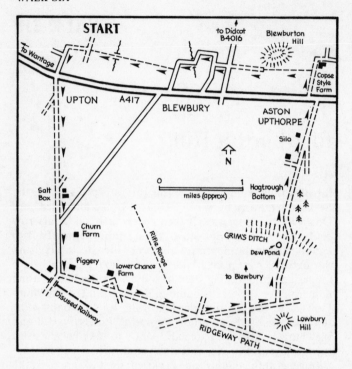

How to get there: The walk is easily reached from the surrounding towns. Take the A417, from Wantage or Rowstock if you approach from the west, or from Streatley if coming from the east. As you pass through Upton, take one of the several lanes running to the north and into the village, where you should be able to find suitable parking space without too much difficulty. For convenience I have suggested that the walk starts from Upton Manor House.

The Walk: Start near Upton Manor House. Walk to the Reading-Wantage road (A417), and take the lane across the road signposted to Alden Farm. You ascend gently in a gully. At the top of the slope the road forks. Bear left up a muddy cart track, recessed between hedges and mature trees.

The track emerges in due course on open downland and passes straight ahead, mostly as a grassy path. The occasional skylark, peewit or hare may cross your path, but there is little else, for this area of downland is very open and can be extremely bleak.

The grass track soon joins a cement farm road from the left. Soon passing a white bungalow and larger house on the left, called Salt Box, you keep ahead. It is a long straight road which is joined by a further road from the left by a water pumping station. As you pass the turning to Churn Farm, on the left, a large barn and railway bridge come into view slightly on the right. The bridge is on the disused Didcot, Newbury and Winchester line opened in 1882. Its construction was much favoured by Lord Wantage; it connected isolated farms on the Downs and at Churn Halt, and gave direct access to the rifle ranges. Lord Wantage was not only a keen and active shot, but as president of the National Rifle Association, founded the Loyd-Lindsay Prize at Bisley.

On the corner is a white bungalow. Turn left along the track; pass a piggery and Lower Chance Farm. At the farm, the cement track bears left and a grass road runs ahead, which you follow, passing gallops and rifle range on the left.

Walk ahead to the Ridgeway Path, which, in a muddle of scissor crossing paths, is clearly signposted, and follow it for 100 yards, then bear gently left off the Ridge Way and slightly uphill. Take care with this junction: It is all too easy to miss the correct track. You follow this straight track for about 800 yards when you cross the broad grass expanse of a wide track which runs down to Woodway Farm and Blewbury on the left, and to Roden Downs on the right.

Lowbury Hill, a low, round eminence, appears half right. At its summit is a triangulation station and the outline of a rectangular enclosure which has been dated to late Roman times (4th century AD). See also the historical note on page 40.

In a further 300 yards or so from the Blewbury Lane, take a somewhat indistinct track to the left which gently descends and curves to the right. In a few steps it becomes a well defined track, but it is easy to miss at the start.

The track runs downhill and a distinct hollow forms to the right. You pass one of the few downland dew ponds on the left, and the track then swings left and right through the line of a Grim's Ditch, one of those pre-Roman linear earthworks.

You run down a spur with two valleys converging from left and right. The track then plunges into Hogtrough Bottom. Wooded slopes rise to the right covered in juniper and conifers. Nearby is a reserve of the Berkshire, Buckinghamshire and Oxfordshire Naturalists' Trust which is notable for its butterflies and junipers; quail and stone curlews frequent this area in summer. In winter the track hereabouts is exceptionally muddy for some distance along the bottom.

After nearly half a mile you pass an isolated bungalow to the left, and a drier road by-passes some of the mud. At a grain silo and barn on the left, a metalled road begins which you follow for $3/4$ mile to the A417. Walk over the cross road towards Aston Upthorpe. Pass Copse Style Farm on the right, and where the road turns sharply right round the corner of farm outbuildings, take a footpath on the left. It runs between fences along a field boundary, with an orchard to the right. In 200 yards you cross a mature track which runs back to Aston. Keep ahead along a path which is very easy to follow. You soon pass Blewburton Hill on the right, at the far end of which a footpath runs sharply uphill to the oval camp on the summit (see historical notes). Should you wish to make this detour, it will afford you a magnificent view.

It is now half a mile of straight, and at times muddy, track to the Didcot road on the eastern edge of Blewbury. Cross the road and walk ahead into the village, in 300 yards turning right at the T-junction. Follow the road round the outside of the village. It turns left, crosses a stream, passes a shop on the left, then turns sharply left.

In about 250 yards on the right, by a yellow fire hydrant post, is the signposted footpath which passes over the fields to Upton. In threequarters of a mile you cross by a bridge over one of the tributaries of Mill Brook, which will eventually flow into the Thames just below Wallingford. In a further 400 yards you cross a track on the outskirts of the village. Follow the orchard on the left, and within a few steps you are back at Upton Manor, where the walk began.

Historical Notes:

Upton: A small village under the Downs with an ancient flint-faced church dating largely from Norman times, but partly from Saxon: the North doorway is Saxon, while the South doorway and massive chancel arch are Norman.

Churn Range: This rifle range, high on the bleak, open Downland above Upton and Blewbury, was opened towards the end of the last century at the instigation of Lord Wantage, a keen shot and a pioneer of the Territorial Volunteers. The range is accessible by road from the north but also formerly by rail on the Didcot, Newbury and Southampton line of 1882, with a small station at Churn Halt. This site became, in summer months up to and during the Great War, a substantial tented army camp.

Aston Tirrold & Upthorpe: Aston Tirrold is a pretty village with an ancient church with Saxon and Norman parts. But of equal interest is the Independent Chapel said to date from 1670. If authentic, this is highly remarkable, for the Nonconformists would not have been able to worship at all at that date. Aston Upthorpe is just about a continuation of Tirrold. The church, with a Norman font, maintains the tradition that it was here that King Ethelred heard Mass before the great Battle of Ashdown in 871. However, Asser's description of this Mass indicates that Ethelred heard the service in a tent, suggesting that the tradition may indeed be erroneous.

Blewburton Hill: This is a massive outlier of chalk lying between Aston Upthorpe and Blewbury, but with interesting strip lynchets around it and a substantial and magnificent Iron Age fort and earthworks on its relatively flat summit. Occupation of the fort was sporadic between 350BC and about 50AD. It is possible that it was brought to a terrible end by the advancing Roman armies after their invasion of Britain. Considerable evidence of violence, destruction, and burning was found during excavation. Unfortunately there it no precise dating evidence to confirm this and the tragedy could have occurred a few years earlier.

Blewbury: This is Rev. Morgan Jones' village. Nick-named 'Blewbury Jones', he has been immortalised by Dickens in 'Our Mutual Friend', as a miser who wore the same coat for 42 years until it was just shreds and tatters. Curate Jones is reputed to have stolen a scarecrow's hat because it was better than his own, and he lived on $12\frac{1}{2}$p a week, which he is said to have spent on two necessities, bread and milk, and one luxury, tea!

The Malthus School, opposite the church, was founded by

money left by a Reading Merchant who traded in timber, namely Thomas Malthus. In 1709 the school was opened for educating the poor of the village. Boys were taught on the ground floor, and the girls upstairs. Beside the master and mistress, a weaver was employed to teach the children work, and attached to the school was its own workhouse.

Lowbury Hill: See Fairmile walk.

The Fairmile and Unhill Bottom

Introduction: If you like walking, it is axiomatic that you will enjoy and appreciate the countryside. This walk, on the Streatley portion of the Downs close to the Goring Gap, is in surely one of the most distinctive and varied parts of upland southern England. You may very well decide to spent most of the day in the area of this walk, there is so much of interest in landscape, vegetation and walking conditions. The Fairmile itself is a broad expanse of springy, soft, turf which extends for over a mile across the Cholsey Downs between Kingstanding Hill and Lowbury Hill. It can easily be reached by car from the main road and is a superb picnic spot where the whole family can relax and play in complete security — and enjoy the delights of a deeply undulating landscape, here wooded, there open, elsewhere arable or maybe covered in the rough grassland characteristic of the Downs.

From Kingstanding Hill and the Fairmile the walk reaches the summit of the Downs, in this area at about 600 feet, near Lowbury Hill, then curves round to the east to join one of the Ridgeway Paths for a short distance near Warren Farm, before branching down through Ham Wood and Unhill Wood, and finally, gently descending Unhill Bottom to near the foot of Kingstanding Hill again.

Distance: Some 5½-6 miles. Allow a minimum of 2 hours to complete the walk, but longer if you intend to make the detour to the top of Lowbury Hill or dwell in the woodland above Unhill Bottom.

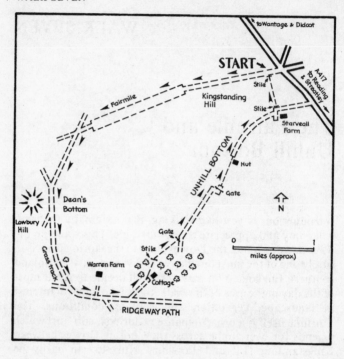

Refreshments: There are no pubs on the route of the walk itself, but several good ones in nearby Streatley. I would recommend anyone to take a picnic with them since the whole area is excellent for settling down, having a quiet bite and a drink from a flask, and just enjoying the wonderful view.

How to get there: The walk is best reached via the A417 from Blewbury, three miles away, or Streatley, which is two miles in the other direction. Alternatively you can get to the start of the walk by minor road from Wallingford through Cholsey to Kingstanding Hill (MR 573838). From the Blewbury direction turn right up the rough track at Kingstanding Hill. You can either stop near the junction with the A417 or continue for half a mile up the gentle slope and park on the Fairmile. Whichever course you decide to take, the walk can begin right there.

The Walk: From the bottom of Kingstanding Hill you will find the slope quite an easy one up this wide pebble and flint track. There is woodland to the right and, through the hedgerows, excellent views open up to the left over Starveall Farm on Moulsford Bottom and, behind you, across to the Chilterns. At one point the track narrows running between high hedges, then suddenly opens and splits into three parallel tracks over a width of some 50 yards of soft turf. This is the Fairmile, which continues straight as a die for just over a mile ahead. There are good views to left and right of wooded hilltops, for you are walking along one ridge among several others, in this highly dissected piece of downland. It is a place for the naturalist; there is a wealth of plants and in summer months, butterflies, the Meadow Brown and Marbled White predominating.

At the end of the Fairmile you bear along a narrower flint-covered track. The round eminence of Lowbury Hill dominates the sky-line ahead and slightly to the right, while the expanse of Dean's Bottom lies to the left. The track rises gradually and passes through beech and hawthorns, slightly bending to the left. If you wish to take in the summit of Lowbury Hill then make a slight detour at this point.

In order to continue the walk, you then leave the hedge on your left and the track crosses open country giving wide views over the Vale of Aylesbury, to the Hampshire Downs ahead and to the Ilsley and Hendred Downs on the right. Warren Farm, around which the walk circles, lies half-left.

In a matter of yards, take a narrower grass-covered track ahead which leads to a lone hawthorn treee at which the track bears left.

Ahead, a large ash tree marks the spot where the grass track is joined from the right, by a flint-covered track which is in fact part of the long-distance Ridgeway path.

You pass the turning to Warren Farm on the left in 400 yards and in a further 150 yards' walk ahead, a track branches right to Aldworth.

Three hundred yards from the Aldworth turn, bear left and enter Town Copse.

You enter the wood through gates with a cottage to the right. It is very easy to miss the path from this point although painted arrows on the beech trees help to guide the walker.

You walk along the cottage garden boundary, which is an earthen embankment, and through the wood for about 400 yards.

On a hot day the cool and scent of the beech wood is a welcome relief to the blasting heat outside. Near the edge of the wood you cross an old stile and keep straight on.

A wide field gateway on the right has an arrow indicating you to pass through it. Walk down the field boundary to your left keeping the fence on your left. This section of footpath is rather overgrown and can be wet, and increasingly runs downhill.

At the end of the field you cross a fence and the white arrow tells you to take the track which you have joined and walk to the left with the field boundary on your left. You are again walking downhill and, at a prominent beech tree, the path bears right.

For some 30 yards you walk uphill then turn right walking downhill for about 50 yards to a gateway on the left through which you pass.

You will now find yourself on the right of a very large field running down the centre of Unhill Bottom. Keep the fence to your right until you come to a metal shed.

You now follow the centre of Unhill Bottom through the middle of the field which is in fact a track.

In something like half-a-mile, Starveall Farm comes into sight. It has an interesting name and is derived from a belief that the land was no good at all and was consequently aptly named "Starve All."

Very soon the track through the field joins a flint road from the right. Keep ahead for about 60 yards, then cross the stile to the left and walk obliquely over the pasture on the left.

There is a well-defined track through the field. Once over the field, keep the hedge to the right and cross the stile to join the road at the bottom of Kingstanding Hill where the walk began.

Historical Notes:

Lowbury Hill: It has a Roman camp at its summit. It is dated to 4th century AD but, although of typically rectangular shape, it is not thought to have had any military purpose. However there may have been an earlier Iron Age camp on the site. The Romans scattered so many oyster shells hereabouts that it is known in the area as Oyster Hill. The view from the summit is wide, over to Compton and Aldworth on the south, and down the deep valley of Unhill Bottom to the north-east. It is well worth the additional climb to the summit.

Starveall: A farm name repeated twice within three miles in the area of the walk and referring to farmland which was considered to be completely unproductive, meaning for the farmer and his family a 'starve all' life.

Kingstanding Hill: The name points to a tradition that here, near the site of the Battle of Ashdown in 871, King Alfred and his Saxon army pitched their tents.

Fairmile: It runs from the foot of Lowbury for over a mile. It is a magnificent greensward track, completely straight and even, and some 45 feet in width. This is the West Icknield way, one of the branches of the Ridgeway which issues off the Downs to reach the Lower Icknield Way at the foot of Kingstanding Hill.

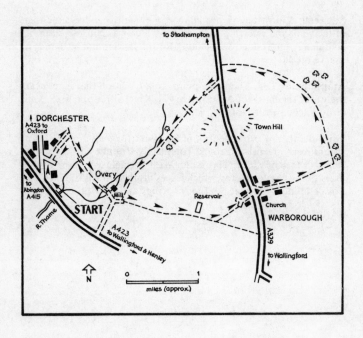

Dorchester

Introduction: This walk begins at Dorchester, passes through Overy and Warborough, and takes in gently rolling country near Berrick Salome and Drayton St Leonard. This is the Vale of Oxfordshire, the lush claylands which lie beneath the green, tree-clade escarpment of the Chiltern Hills some five miles to the east. Not far away, and easily visible from the walk, the Chilterns and Berkshire Downs pinch the River Thames at Goring and Streatley to force it through the impressively scenic gap into the lower Thames Valley at Reading and Maidenhead.

But here, in the middle Thames Valley is a distinctive and wonderful walking country. It is dominated by Dorchester, a Roman town, with a considerable Abbey Church and many quaint by-ways sheltering pretty cottages and more substantial houses. Overy, a mile or so away has one of the best examples of a village mill anywhere in this district, while Warborough is a spacious settlement spread out around extensive greens and open spaces, the cottages and inns exhibiting an inimitable charm.

Distance: The circuit is about five miles and should take under three hours to complete, but if you dwell in your visit to Dorchester Abbey (and you ought to) it will naturally take longer. Please note also that this walk was written up before the construction of the Dorchester by-pass which crosses the route. Its arrival will cause inconvenience but should not alter the overall safety or enjoyment of the walk.

Refreshments: There are numerous inns and several restaurants in Dorchester, while at Warborough, if the time

43

is right, you may decide to call at the good pubs there. There is ample space and several suitable sites for picnics to be found on the course of the walk.

How to get there: Dorchester is on the A423 Oxford to Henley road and the walk begins at Dorchester Abbey.

The walk: You start at Dorchester Abbey. Pass through the lych gate into the churchyard. In summer months the museum on the left is open, and is housed in the old monastery guest house dating from about 1400. Take a look inside the Abbey, particularly at the wall painting, the great east window and the lead font.

Walk past the tower beside the old cloister garden. The gravel lane curves to the left. In a few steps, at a junction of drives, take the narrow footpath with a high brick wall on the right, which lies half-right. It issues on to a road which you take ahead for about a hundred yards, where it ends at a track. Turn right along this cart track, in 120 yards crossing a bridge and stile into open fields.

Ahead lies Overy Mill on the River Thame. This is one of the most picturesque mills in the district. It had a double water wheel, in effect working two mills, and the prosperity of the enterprise in the 18th and 19th centuries is surely attested to by the considerable extent and overall proportions of the miller's living quarters.

The footpath passes in front of the mill and through the garden. At the road junction in 25 yards bear left and walk for 350 yards passing under the bypass bridge. After this turn right and proceed for approximately 700 yards along the field side of the bypass. Then bear left towards the right hand side of a reservoir surrounded by trees. About 200 yards further on, a vertically mounted stone slab on the left marks the point where a footpath branches from the track across the field to Warborough. If you aim for the prominent tower of the church on the skyline, you will keep to the right path.

You enter Warborough over the field by way of a narrow footpath into a housing area. Follow the road ahead to the village shop opposite the church. Take a look inside the church, for here is a second lead font. These are considerable rarities. There are only 36 in all England, and five are in a line from Warborough, to the west, at Dorchester, Long

Wittenham, Sparsholt and Woolstone. Take a look also at the memorial in the chancel to two illustrious members of the Randolph family, Francis and Herbert.

Now follow the road to the left of the church tower; at the junction bear right, passing the pub on the right, then the soccer and cricket pitches with the Six Bells over the greensward. A whole series of pretty cottages and houses run beside the road on the left, which ceases to be metalled and turns into a wide public bridleway ahead, with part of the low eminence of Town Hill coming into view on the left, and the range of the Chilterns now very much clearer, ahead. The bridleway is diverted slightly by turning right and quickly left around a field edge and comes to a stop under power lines at the corner of a square wood. Turn left along a footpath with a deep ditch on the right.

The prominent cream frontage of Ewe Farm lies a miles away on a low hill to the right, and a quarter right an extensive wood bends away from the walk. Continue along the footpath passing a series of dead elms. Pass through a hedge into the next field, leaving behind you the end of the wood on the right. The path curves gently left round the base of Town Hill. You pass through another hedge into the next field, and in due course cross a gate beside a small copse which issues on to a road. Turn left for 70 yards, then take the obvious public bridleway on the right. In a short distance the track narrows down and you pass piggeries on the left with the open valley of the River Thame on the right, with views to Berinsfield and rising ground in the distance near Garsington.

When you have passed the piggeries, the track continues up a line of willows and ends at a power line which crosses the track. Ahead lies an open grass track which ends with a copse and the River Thame on the right, and a broad track running down from Warborough on the left. Walk ahead, keeping the River Thame on the right, then crossing a stile into a pasture, keeping the field boundary on the right. Walk under the bypass and after 360 yards turn right to pass in front of Overy Mill. It is now simple to follow the path back to Dorchester Abbey, where the walk began.

Historical Notes:

Dorchester: is in reality one of England's oldest cities, although today it is hardly more than a village. It was an important town in Roman times associated with a river crossing and on a Roman road running from Alcester to Silchester. The place was also twice the seat of a bishopric, first as the cathedral city of Wessex, later as that of Mercia, forming parts of the sees of Winchester then Lincoln. In 1140 the Bishop of Lincoln founded a Priory of Austin Canons here, endowing them with most of the valuable possessions of the bishopric, so the Cathedral became in effect Dorchester's Abbey Church. At the dissolution of the Abbeys it was fortunately saved, being purchased by a townsman for the princely sum of £140. In his will he left the building to the parish of Dorchester. Through the Lych Gate lies the old schoolroom which is now a museum and is all that remains of the Priory buildings. Outside the south door of the church is a good churchyard cross, well restored, and evidently saved from the depredations of the Puritans.

Inside the Abbey is a fine lead font, one of five in Oxfordshire out of only 36 in all England. It has rich effigies of 11 apostles standing under canopies. Mediaeval ochre wall-paintings can be seen beyond the font.

The fine windows at the east end of the Abbey, particularly the Jesse window, should be examined. Jesse is a recumbent figure at the foot, and from his body spring the branches of the tracery, forming a genealogical tree, with stone figures at intervals. The brilliant painted glass figures also form part of this unique scheme.

The south chancel has tombs to John Stonor (1354), Chief Justice; Lord Segrove, Governor of Wallingford Castle (1400); an unknown knight and an unknown bishop.

Overy: just between Dorchester and Warborough lies on the river Thame. A few substantial houses form the hamlet which surrounds one of the finest watermills in this part of Oxfordshire. It is a double mill, with a fine attached mill house, quite clearly extended to the east probably to accommodate the miller's son. The whole structure is picturesque and substantial.

Warborough: A fine village surrounding an extensive village green. The church here also has a lead font and is very similar to the third font in the area at Long Wittenham, in that it is much more simple in design than that at Dorchester. Broadly the church is largely Early English, showing the remains of a rood loft, and a tower which is dated 1666.

WALK NINE

Long Wittenham and the Pendon Museum

Introduction: This is a short walk which begins at Appleford and passes over flat and pretty countryside to Long Wittenham. You pass down the length of this ancient and quaint village, then over the bridleways and footpaths to the side of the Thames which you will follow upsteam to Clifton Hampden Bridge. From there you return to Appleford by a combination of road and footpath. A particularly enjoyable feature of this walk can be a visit to the Pendon Museum at Long Wittenham. It is thoroughly recommended and involves almost no deviation from the route of the walk. See notes for times of opening.

Distance: Some $4^3/_4$ miles, and should take you about two hours. Most times of the year it is important that you wear suitable footwear against water and mud on this walk, for the riverine footpaths can be tacky even at the height of summer.

Refreshments: There are several inns on the route including the Machine Man, the Vine and the Plough at Long Wittenham and the Barley Mow at Clifton Hampden Bridge. This latter inn is one of the oldest in the area and is now restored, having been gutted by fire. Of course this is the inn made famous by Jerome K Jerome in his 'Three Men in a Boat'.

How to get there: Access to Appleford is by the B4016 from Drayton or Didcot, and from Abingdon by taking the A415 from Abingdon towards Henley and two miles outside

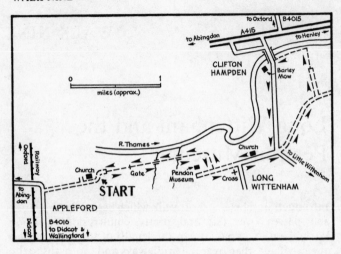

Abingdon turning off to Culham, then in half a mile turning left on to the B4016 to Appleford church which is some two miles further. Appleford Halt is on the main railway line between Oxford and Didcot and very close to the start of the walk, if you decide to come by train.

The Walk: From the church, whose Victorian spire is visible for miles around, take the track which winds round the southern and eastern sides of the churchyard. A finger-post indicates the right-of-way quite clearly and it is easy to follow. From the church the track straightens out along the left edge of a field and is some 50 yards from the River Thames which runs to the left beneath the terrace.

At the end of the field you pass through a metal gate beside a substantial oak tree, then follow the wire fence which you keep to your left. At the end of this field take the white metal bridge which crosses a swiftly flowing stream, then in some 50 yards cross a second footbridge.

The River Thames has now looped round and is only some 15 yards to the left at a point which is much favoured by fishermen. The river now accompanies the footpath for

48

much of its way into Long Wittenham and in a few steps after you have entered the village, the footpath ends at the road. The route now turns left along this road which runs through the village. However the Pendon Museum is now only a couple of hundred yards down the road on the right and is well worth a quick visit.

When you return to the walk, go back up the street and continue ahead. The first house on the left, possibly once a shop, has a small plate high on the wall which announces "By appointment to H.M. King George V," but the reason for the warrant has long since disappeared.

A little further on you pass the ancient village cross on your right at the road junction. You continue ahead and walk along the village street, passing a whole wealth of character-filled cottages and gardens, while on the left is the Plough Inn, and in due course, the Grapes on the right.

On the left you pass the school and church. The former has the shallow remains of a village cock-pit near to it, and the latter is worth closer inspection as it contains one of the few leaden fonts to be found in England.

At the road junction at the far end of the village take the road to Little Wittenham, but in a matter of ten yards turn off it to the left up a narrow metalled road along which points a public footpath sign.

In half a mile on your left the road turns sharply right, then in about 150 yards turn left off the road along a broad grass track clearly indicated as a footpath only. In a further half-mile the track ends and you cross a gate. The right-of-way runs ahead along the fence which you keep to your left.

Across this field you come to the river along the side of which you turn left and follow the towing path to Clifton Hampden Bridge. At the bridge you can either walk over it to explore Clifton Hampden village, or turn left along the road, and passing the Barley Mow Inn on the right, return to Long Wittenham.

The river is a few yards to your right for most of the way, and in less than half-a-mile you pass Clifton Lock on the right. In winter this road is often flooded and the raised wooden pathway on the left quite clearly provides a much-needed service on those occasions.

At the road junction at the north-eastern end of Long

Wittenham, turn right along the village main street and return to Appleford church by way of the footpath.

Historical Notes:

Appleford: A low-lying village wedged between the Didcot to Oxford railway line and the river Thames, having much modern development. There are a number of picturesque houses approaching the church. The church itself was re-built in Victorian times but some old features remain, including two Norman doorways and a curious early font. The distinctive spire of the building is a landmark throughout the district.

Long Wittenham: Although once called Earl's Wittenham, Long Wittenham as it is now known, is quite true to its name, for its main street extends for a considerable distance parallel with the river Thames. There are some fine houses and quaint cottages facing onto the street. Lying back from it, towards the river, is the church with a distinctive lead font in the Baptistry. The building has late Norman and Early English features, but a certain amount of rebuilding has taken place.

There have been considerable archaeological finds in the parish, including an Anglo-Saxon cemetery. One find, a pot with bronze panels, was taken to the British Museum. A Romano-British settlement was discovered in the loop of the Thames near Northfield Farm in about 1893, the buildings constructed wholly of daub and wattle.

Pendon Museum, Long Wittenham: The museum contains wonderfully modelled miniature scenes from the English countryside, in particular of the Vale of the White Horse as they would have been seen in the early 1930s. There is also a considerable amount of Railwayana and a visit will be a delight to all those for whom the initials GWR conjure up the glorious vision of steam, speed and shining brass. The museum is open on Saturday and Sunday afternoons between 2 and 5 pm. Between March and October the hours extend to 6 pm and it opens on Bank Holidays.

Clifton Hampden: The village lies on the opposite side of the river from the walk and can be reached by the ornate bridge of six russet-coloured arches built to designs of Sir George Gilbert Scott in 1864. The surroundings are delightful: long valued by artists, fishermen and visitors alike.

Sunningwell —
Matthew Arnold Country

Introduction: These are two circular walks, one short and one long, which start and finish at the church in Sunningwell, between Oxford and Abingdon. They take in a substantial section of the Cumnor Hills, which overlook the towers and spires of Oxford on one side, and the Vale of the White Horse on the other. They offer wide views, a variety of scenery and excellent good walking country, both wooded and open.

The walks pass through some of the country beloved by Matthew Arnold and referred to at length in his *Scholar Gipsy* and *Thyrsis*. They also pass the artificial hill called Jarn Mound, built up by Sir Arthur Evans, the famous archaeologist, to complete a splendid view over the tree tops to the distant countryside. There is a view indicator on the summit of the mound for the guidance of visitors.

Distance: Either 6 miles or 3¹/₂ miles. In normal conditions the walks should take about 3 hours for the long one and 2 hours for the short one.

Refreshments: Two good inns deserve a visit, namely The Fox on Boar's Hill, and The Flowing Well at Sunningwell. The latter inn has the advantage of an extensive garden, although there are several possible picnic sites on the walk, such as Jarn Mound and Matthew Arnold's field.

How to get there: Sunningwell is just north of Abingdon, but the great A34 trunk road slices between the two and may mean a careful approach to get to the start of the walk at Sunningwell church. From the Oxford direction take the *old*

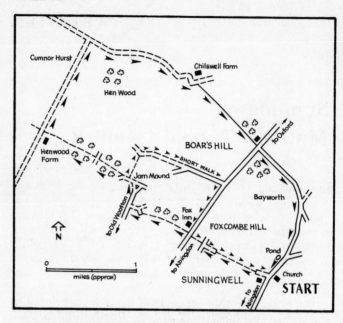

A34 road from the roundabout junction of the Western and Southern ring roads with the Abingdon by-pass. Go up Hinksey Hill and at the top drive straight ahead. In some $3/4$ mile take left turn going steeply down hill through Bayworth to Sunningwell. Alternatively, come into Abingdon and take the Wootton (B4017) Road from the town. Having passed under the by-pass turn right in some 300 yards to the village of Sunningwell.

The walk: Whether you are following the long or the short route, take the lane opposite Sunningwell church which passes alongside the village hall. Crossing a track, you should aim for a white gate at the top of the hillside. Leave the field by a small gate and take a glance at the view behind you. It extends the width of the Vale of the White Horse, and ranges from the Chiltern Hills through Wittenham Clumps to beyond White Horse Hill on the west.

Follow the metalled road ahead for about 500 yards. A

road joins from the left by a post box. Take the narrow path ahead. Crossing a stile in a few yards, the path descends, with an ornamental lake on the left, then begins to rise gently. Emerging on Boar's Hill with the Fox Inn opposite, turn left down the hill for 50 yards, then right along a signposted footpath.

You descend gently along the edge of a field with woodland rising to your right. Crossing a double stile over a stream, the path begins to rise. Cross a further stile and enter the woodland.

The path winds uphill between enclosed gardens and before long widens to a gravel drive and in 100 yards is joined by another drive from the right.

In a further 100 yards you walk on to a metalled road beside Norman Bank, a picturesque thatched cottage on your left. Turn right here and follow the metalled road uphill for 250 yards, when you come to a T-junction at Jarn Mound.

Of course Jarn Mound is artificial and was built by Sir Arthur Evans, the archaeologist, to extend the view to take in White Horse Hill, Red Horse Hill in Warwickshire, Inkpen Beacon, Wychwood Forest and the Chilterns. Some say the Mendips can be seen on the clearest days!

The short walk continues from Jarn Mound and is itemised separately two paragraphs from the end of this text. For those on the longer walk turn left at the T-junction for about 60 yards to Matthew Arnold's Field. It was from here that Arnold took much inspiration for "Thyrsis" and "Scholar Gipsy". Three footpaths are signposted. Take the middle once across Arnold's Field. Excellent views along the corallian ridge extend to Harrowdown Hill below Longworth, Buckland and Faringdon Folly.

Descending across the field, you find a gate leading into a thicket. The path is well defined through gorse, bracken and bramble. At the far end bear right and in due course cross a driveway leading to Black Hill Copse. The path falls and rises over a valley. You cross the metalled road at the top of Wootton Hill and take the unsignposted footpath ahead, ignoring the tempting sign pointing down to the left.

Walk between garden boundaries and woodland for some distance, you cross a footbridge then take the stile ahead into the field beyond, which you cross, taking a further footbridge to the next field, the edge of which you follow, keeping the boundary to your left.

Ita can be very sticky underfoot hereabouts, and it may be a relief to leave the field, emerging into a lane. Henwood Farm is within halooing distance to your left, and shows an interesting variety of architectural styles, from half-hipped roofs to Dutch gabling. Turn right along the lane. Cumnor Hurst is now three-quarters left, and you may find that this mile-long section of the walk will be rather muddy in wet weather.

About half a mile beyond Henwood Farm the path twists slightly under electricity pylons, and with the water tower now ahead on the skyline you follow the track slightly to the right, and in 100 yards take the left turn through a gateway walking for 300 yards to a junction at which you turn right.

It is much drier now, and to your left are wide views over Oxford, unfortunately framed between the clutter of "pendant bluebells" carrying a web of high-voltage cables.

The track contours round the hill to Chilswell Farm. Turn left into the farm and right out of it. Take the stile to the right just beyond the farm, but ignore the indicated footpath in that direction, taking the route which follows the field boundary on your left. Keep the boundary on your left all the time, passing into successive fields. Eventually you will come to a cement field-bridge which lets onto a very narrow field which you cross in 50 yards to a gate. Through the gate you walk for 200 yards on a wide grass verge at the right of another field to a gateway which passes into a wood.

The ascent through the wood is steep and can be wet. You come to a derelict building which you round to your right emerging on a metalled road.

The rest of the walk is easy and will give ample opportunity to clear the mud from your boots. Cross the road and walk down Bayworth Lane ahead. The steep descent leads to Bayworth, where you bear right to Sunningwell, turning right at the Flowing Well Inn to regain the church and the starting point.

The short walk continues from Jarn Mound and is very easy walking. At the T-junction on the south of the mound, take the path ahead which passes to the left of the mound. In 200 yards you come to a metalled road. Turn right along it. In some 500 yards another will join from the right. Just beyond here are excellent views to Oxford and beyond over open ground to the Oxford Preservation Trust.

In about 500 yards you reach the road which has climbed up Boar's Hill. You have the choice of turning right and walking some 700 yards to the Fox Inn and turning left to go back to Sunningwell the same way as you came; or turning left at the junction and walking as far as Bayworth Lane and following the walk indicated two paragraphs back for completion of the six mile route.

Historical Notes:

Sunningwell: The church porch is unique. It is seven-sided and attaches itself at the west of the building. It is supposed to have been built for one of the village's most distinguished Rectors, John Jewel, later Bishop of Salisbury, who died in 1571 and was Rector of Sunningwell about 1551. He had a chequered career in the church, as did many men during that extraordinary period of religious uncertainty. He was quite happy under the reformed church of Henry VIII, but with the accession of Mary and a return to the old Catholic beliefs he fled the country and in 1555 arrived in Frankfurt. The accession of Elizabeth I saw his return, but not to Sunningwell, for he was consecrated Bishop of Salisbury.

Another notable incumbent here was Dr Samuel Fell who became Dean of Christ Church. A staunch monarchist, it was reported that he died grief-striken when told of Charles I's execution. While at Christ Church, the Earl of Pembroke, as Chancellor of Oxford, had the task of turning Royalists from the University. When the Dean's turn came to be evicted, he told Pembroke that . . . "he was too inconsiderable a person for a Dean of Christ Church to parley with." Outraged, the Earl replied by sending Fell to prison, forcibly turning his family from the Deanery.

An even earlier association between Oxford University and Sunningwell was forged through Roger Bacon, and without doubt added to scientific discovery. The famous 13th century scientist was experimenting in Oxford about 1250, and he used Sunningwell church tower to test and perfect his telescope.

Matthew Arnold loved the Cumnor Hills. From footpaths hereabouts he turned to see "The line of festal light in Christ Church Hall" from his favoured "warm, green-muffled Cumnor Hills". The walks take in Powder Hill Copse and pass close to Childsworth Farm, the likely site of the Signal Elm, Cumnor Hurst, and cross the celebrated Happy Valley, which run s from the Hills to South Hinksey and Oxford.

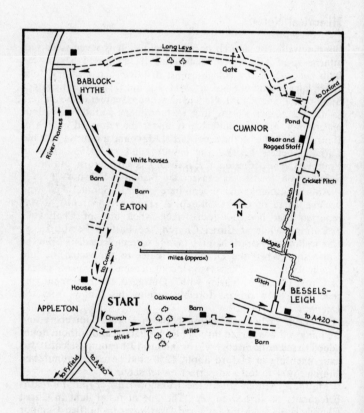

Appleton, Cumnor and Bablock Hythe

Introduction: 'The village surrounded by apple orchards' is what the place name means. Appleton is an admirable place to begin this varied and attractive walk. It passes through woodland and parkland to Bessels Leigh, then over arable fields to Cumnor. You take an engaging walk from Cumnor, along a track called the Long Leys, to Bablock Hythe, at a former ferry point over the river Thames. This was a route which Matthew Arnold travelled on his local walks and his reference in "Scholar Gipsy" to:

> 'Thee at the ferry Oxford riders blithe,
> Returning home on summer nights, have met
> Crossing the stripling Thames at Bablock Hythe
> Trailing in the cool stream they fingers wet,
> As the punt's rope chops round.' . . .

will be familiar to many.

From the river you walk a quiet and now dead-end lane to Eaton, then take a field footpath back to Appleton.

Distance: The circular route is about 6½ miles in all, and should take between three and four hours to complete.

Refreshments: There are ample inns along the route, should you wish that kind of refreshment. There is the Thatched Tavern, The Plough and the Three Horseshoes at Appleton. The Greyhound at Bessels Leigh, The Bear and Ragged Staff at Cumnor and the Eight Bells at Eaton — so you are well provided for. Picnics can suitably be taken in Appleton Wood or between Cumnor and the river at Bablock Hythe.

How to get there: Take the A420 from Faringdon or Oxford and the A338/A415 from Wantage and Abingdon. Access to Appleton village is from the A420 dual carriageway in Tubney Wood and very close to the Bessels Leigh junction with the A338. It is clearly signposted.

The Walk: This walk begins at Appleton church and you start by walking along its western and southern sides, then following the footpath through the churchyard which runs due east. Cross the gate and stile from the church yard, walk ahead over 50 yards of pasture then cross a further stile and follow the very well defined footpath ahead which keeps the field fence on the right.

In due course cross the footbridge into the beautiful oak wood of Bessels Leigh Common through which you pass for some 300 yards on a newly maintained gravel path through the bracken, emerging from the wood over a stile.

The footpath lies ahead along the right side of a long and narrow field. In 500 yards you are level with barns on the left and you cross a stile on to a gravelled farm road ahead. At the green barn turn left for 200 yards to the road along which you turn right walking through Bessels Leigh.

Turn up the lane beside Home Farm Cottage on the left and pass into the field beyond, walking ahead and keeping the ditch to the left. The footpath from Appleton to Bessels Leigh is spendidly clear and well maintained; but from Bessels Leigh to Cumnor it is a somewhat different story, and great care is necessary in finding the route.

When the ditch turns left walk ahead across the field aiming for the corner of the hedgerow opposite. Now follow the hedgerow up the field keeping it to your right.

In the corner of the field the path passes through the hedge. You must cross the ditch without the aid of a footbridge, but there was no water in it when I passed that way recently. As a further guide, you are directly under high voltage power cables at this point.

You now walk ahead up a ploughed field, keeping the hedge to your left. In due course the hedge turns left for a distance, then right again for some 400 yards. At this point where the hedge turns left the path goes ahead up the field and you should aim for the hedge again some 400 yards ahead, where it shelters a stream.

Follow the stream. As a guide, there is a distinctively tall poplar tree on the edge of Cumnor just to the right of the line of walk. The path now becomes much better defined.

At the end of the field a very wide lane opens ahead, up which you pass, with the village cricket square on the right. You now enter Cumnor and walk up the road ahead, passing the Bear and Ragged Staff on the left.

At the end of the pond bear left and take the path ahead between white metal posts. Take the stile some 40 yards along the lane on the left, and walk up the very long close of pasture keeping the hedge to the left. Go over the stile at the end into an L-shaped football field, keeping the hedge to the right.

A delightful thatched cottage appears on the right in the corner of the field where you go over a fence and turn right along a lane which soon takes you on to a road beside another thatched cottage with 1727 carved on the front.

Turn left along the metalled lane which dips away to give good views over Wytham Woods, Farmoor, the upper Thames and the backslope of the Cotswolds.

It is a gentle walk downhill. In due course take the gateway ahead, where the road bears right, and walk down the Long Leys, a track through a field of pasture, very narrow and virtually 1,000 yards long. Certainly it is aptly named.

Halfway down the slope of Long Leys you pass under a super-grid line, then by an orchard and cottages on the left. At the end of Long Leys the track swings left and changes its character. It is no longer a dry, open, stony track, but becomes narrow, enclosed and in places deeply muddy.

This footpath opens out to a track shortly before it joins the road at Bablock Hythe. It is now a road which goes nowhere, as the ferry over the river is closed. It serves a couple of isolated cottages and the fishermen who use this part of the upper Thames.

Turn left along the road, which for some distance accompanies the river then swings left and uphill over Eaton Heath to Eaton village. You enter the village and very quickly find the indicated footpath on the right opposite a row of white houses. Turn up this track which gives views over the upper Thames to the right. At the poplar trees walk ahead along what is now a footpath at a field edge with the hedge on the right.

In due course the path swings with the hedge to the left and joins the road. Here you turn right and very quickly walk in to Appleton, where the walk began.

Historical Notes:

Appleton: A fine village with a splendid church and manor together with the remains of moats to another two substantial houses. The church is largely late Norman and Early English. Take a look at the brass to John Goodrington and his wife (1518) and the excellent Elizabethan monument to Sir John Fettiplace of 1593. The Fettiplace family took the manor by marriage to the Bessels family but sold it about 1600. The Manor House, close to the church, has Norman and Early English fragments, with an especially fine round-headed doorway leading into the Hall.

Bessels Leigh: This hamlet takes its name from the Bessels family who obtained the estate by marriage in 1350. It was Sir Peter Bessels, he died in 1424, who provided money for building Culham and Abingdon bridges. From the Bessels' the estate passed to the Fettiplaces, then in 1634 to Sir William Lenthall, Speaker in the Long Parliament. The manor house has long since been destroyed.

Cumnor: The manor was owned by Abingdon Abbey as a summer residence and sanatorium. It was given by Henry VIII to the last Abbot, Thomas Rowland, as a reward for leaving Abingdon Abbey so promptly at the dissolution. Cumnor Place, as it came to be called, passed to the ownership of Anthony Forster in 1560. Reputedly it was haunted by the ghost of Amy Robsart. Finally the house, which stood west of the church, was pulled down in 1810 by Lord Abingdon. The story of Amy Robsart has been told many times. Briefly, she was married to Lord Robert Dudley, Earl of Leicester. It was rumoured that Queen Elizabeth would have married him had it not been for Amy. She died at Cumnor when the servants had been sent away to Abingdon fair. She may have been strangled then flung down the stairs breaking her neck. Sir Walter Scott took up the story of Amy Robsart in Kenilworth and enlarged upon it.

Inside the church a fine statue of Elizabeth I is alongside correspondence referring to the Robsart saga. Anthony Forster's elegant monument is on the north side of the chancel.

Fyfield and Appleton Woods

Introduction: If you want a round walk, ideal for any time of the year, but perhaps especially for the early Spring, then take this one. The walk begins at Fyfield, a delightfully unspoilt village close to the A420 between Oxford and Faringdon, and passes through deep woodland, largely a mixture of Oak and Ash in Appleton Lower Common Wood, over open meadow and along towing paths beside the 'stripling' Thames, here more correctly called the Isis. It is a walk full of variety and for the observant walker has an abundance of wildlife.

Before setting off, take a look inside Fyfield church. It is the *memento mori* tomb of Sir John Golafre in the north aisle which is of interest, for he made this village, re-building the church in the 14th century and erecting part of the splendid manor house.

Distance: The full walk is five miles and since it is quite easy going may take the average walker $2\frac{1}{2}$ hours or so. But if you are short of time or want to cover less ground, it can be suitably shortened by taking only the first section making a distance of just three miles.

Refreshments: There is one inn on the route, namely the White Hart at Fyfield, which is itself an historic and picturesque building.

How to get there: The walk begins at Fyfield village green, which is adjacent to the church and the ancient manor house. Fyfield is easily approached along the A420 Swindon to Oxford road, just outside Kingston Bagpuize.

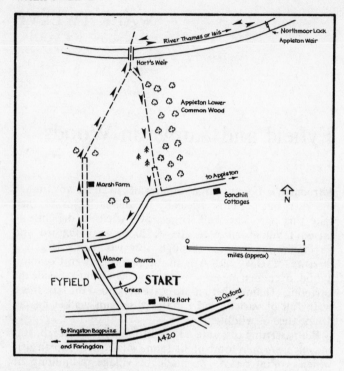

The walk: From the church walk to the road and turn right along it beside the manor wall. The road winds and gently undulates, passing numerous cottages and houses still set in large gardens and orchards. The area bears the stamp of pre 1914 spaciousness, and the hamlet of Netherton is largely unspoiled by later infilling.

Beyond Netherton the metalled road ends beside barns at a T-junction. Walk ahead taking the bridle road. You go slightly uphill passing Marsh Farm on the right — a good example of 19th century enclosure farm — to the edge of the corralian escarpment just beyond the farm.

At this point wide views extend over the Upper Thames Valley, close in masked to some extent by North Audley Copse and Appleton Common Wood, to left and right respectively.

The walk continues as a footpath bearing right and gently downhill, passing diagonally across fields for 700 yards to a line of pylons and overhead power lines. On your right is the corner of Appleton Lower Common Wood.

Depending not only on the time of the year but also the time of day, this woodland has abundant birdlife. In some thickets hereabouts I have tape-recorded nightingales in full song, also seen snipe and cuckoos and the lesser spotted woodpecker, while in other parts of the woodland grow a profusion of honeysuckle and orchids.

You are now aiming for Hart's Weir and the grey wooden footbridge over the river. It soon comes into view. You may be lucky enough to catch a fleeting glimpse of a kingfisher darting along the river hereabouts. Coots, moorhens, and swans are usually in abundance.

At the high bridge and Hart's Weir, retrace your steps, then follow the footpath across a narrow pasture to the pylon at the corner of Appleton Common Wood. You can extend the walk by crossing the high footbridge and turning right. Follow the towing path, here and there crossing small ditches and walking through narrow wooden gates, until you reach Northmoor Lock. You might be able to get an ice cream or some sweets here in the summer, and the walk makes a pleasant riverside ramble, before the time comes to turn round and retrace you steps to Hart's Weir.

Whichever you decide, the final part of the route returns you to Fyfield, taking the path along the edge of Appleton Common Wood, to your left.

Cross a stile and in a hundred yards pass through a narrow gate into the depth of the woodland. It is mixed deciduous wood to the left having a carpet of bluebells, primroses or snow-white anemones in their various flowering periods; dark conifers lie to the right.

The tunnel pathway joins the road near Sandhill Cottages. Turn right and follow the road for half a mile, then turn left into Netherton and return to Fyfield.

Historical Notes:

Fyfield: The Church was burnt down in 1893 but only the observant eye will note the change for the careful restoration retains several 13th century portions in the nave, namely three ancient doorways. They were themselves retained during an earlier restoration in the 14th century when the building was substantially rebuilt by Sir John Golafre, Lord of the Manor, who died in 1363. The following century, another Sir John Golafre, who died in 1442 and was grandson of the former, rebuilt the north aisle intending it to be used as a Chantry.

Tombs of interest are those of George Gale, Fellow of Oriel and Principal of St Mary's Hall, Oxford (1625), a splendid Tudor tomb under a rich canopy said to commemorate Lady Catherine Gordon, the White Rose of Scotland and widow of Perkin Warbeck. She had three other husbands, the last being Christopher Ashfield of Fyfield. She died here in 1527.

The Golafre chapel contains the magnificent tomb of Sir John Golafre the younger. It was Sir John who founded a hospital here and was also a substantial benefactor of Abingdon Bridge.

The Manor House next to the church was originally built in 1325 by Sir John Golafre the elder, but has been much added to since then. The oldest parts are the entrance hall and solar.

The White Hart Inn is 15th century and represents the Chantry building with Priest's house attached founded by Sir John Golafre. The Hall runs to the full height of the house which dimension is retained in the bars.

Fyfield Elm stood on the A420 near Tubney but has succumbed to time and the elements. It is immortalized in the Matthew Arnold's lines:

"Maidens who from distant hamlets come
To dance around the Fyfield Elm in May."

The Upper Thames at Newbridge

Introduction: The walk starts and finishes at Newbridge, one of the river Thames' most ancient and picturesque crossing points, and the site of a brief but violent clash between the armies of the Civil War in 1644.

Notable for variety of landscape, this walk has a considerable attraction as walking country with a superb range of views. It takes in riverside pasture over the Oxford clays, but also a low upland escarpment of the limestone ridge which runs from Oxford to Faringdon and beyond. The ridge lies just south of the upper Thames valley, and divides it from the Vale of the White Horse, which extends south beyond the slope.

Distance: This is a two-part circuit giving a long and a shorter walk. The full walk is about 4 miles and should take $1^1/_2$-2 hours to complete. Add whatever time you spend in Longworth. The shorter 3 mile circuit misses Longworth Village.

Refreshments: There are two good pubs at Newbridge. On the southern side of the river, the Maybush is a simple roadside inn, while the more extensive Rose Revived on the northern side of the river, is a restaurant and hotel also. The Blue Boar at Longworth is very convenient, half-way round the longer walk.

How to get there: From Kingston Bagpuize, on the main Oxford-Swindon road, take the A415 towards Witney. In two miles you come to Newbridge, and in the area of the

65

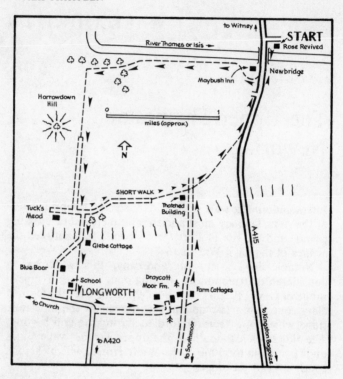

Rose Revived you should be able to find sufficient parking space.

The Walk: Turn right at the southern end of the Maybush and cross a bridge and gate into the pasture beyond, following the towpath upstream. At the end of the field you cross a stile into a further pasture, then a stile into a rougher field. The path runs slightly away from the riverside and above it, because some higher land here gives a steep bank to the river. Follow the edge of the field leaving a small copse between you and the river.

In the corner of the field the track clearly runs ahead and you cross a wooden fence by an oak tree. A shelter belt of trees runs up from your left. Keep walking ahead. The eminence of Harrowdown Hill comes into full view across to the left. You are now walking high above the river which swings north away to your right. Keep walking ahead to the end of the field where you turn left along the field boundary.

You now walk slightly uphill to Harrowdown Hill. At the top of the field pass through a gate and along the footpath ahead which runs on the left of a shelter belt, and is deeply muddy, but this is the right-of-way.

From here there are good views to the left along the ridge towards Appleton and out to Cumnor and the Wytham Hills. When you have rounded the left side of Harrowdown Hill there is a good view ahead to Longworth on top of the ridge.

The footpath has turned into a bridleway and is quite clearly defined ahead. At Tuck's Mead on the right turn left along the lane for 25 yards, and if you should wish to take the shortened walk continue ahead along this track, which in due course bears left and degenerates into a footpath and re-emerges on to the main walk at a thatched livestock shed in the corner of a field. See end of penultimate paragraph.

But for the main walk turn right just after Tuck's Mead up a semi-metalled road. Below Glebe Cottage on the left, the road bears right and runs uphill.

At the top end of the cottage turn left and take the indicated footpath. You cross a stile and walk along the edge of a field with an extensive orchard, then the school field on your right. There are good views behind you back over the Upper Thames.

At the corner of the school field turn right, pass through a metal gate, turn left down Bow Bank, a road running through a small housing area and into the main village street of Longworth. Turn left along it. In a few yards you pass Marten's Hall Farm on the right, recalling Sir Henry Marten of Longworth, one of the signatories of Charles I's death warrant.

Where the road turns right walk ahead up the dusty track, and at the end of the houses continue ahead on the track at the edge of the field. It is a good track. You pass a pond and farm on your right, and in due course Draycott Moor Farm on the left.

At the chestnuts by the outbuildings walk ahead up the

short path which runs between conifers, then turn left along the indicated bridleway, which for 100 yards is a metalled road, then keep going gently downhill along a dusty track. In half-a-mile you come to the thatched livestock shed on the left where the shortened walk re-joins.

Here you turn half-right through a metal gate along an indicated bridleway. Follow the edge of the pasture and keep the hedge on your left. Cross a gate into a further pasture, pass under the electricity wires, follow the hedgerow where it bears left to the end of the field, then turn right for 100 yards to a narrow gate which leads on to the Kingston Bagpuize to Witney road. Turn left along the road, and it is a very short step back to the Rose Revived where the walk began.

Historical Notes:

Newbridge: In spite of its name, it is one of the oldest crossings of the Thames. It dates from the 13th century, and bridges the river at its junction with the Windrush. The bridge, built in honey-coloured limestone, has five pointed arches and triangular buttresses facing upstream. The crossing point was important in the Civil War. In 1644 the bridge was held for the King and attacked by Sir William Waller for parliament, who forced a passage on 2nd June 1644, the immediate result of which was King Charles' night retreat from Oxford. General Waller's men overpowered the guards at Newbridge and obtained boats to put over his forces. The following day he ferried across some 5,000 horse- and foot-soldiers, taking part of that army on, with cannon, to Abingdon.

The Rose Revived Inn stood once as the Rose Inn opposite the Maybush. But having been burnt down, the new Rose was built as the Rose Revived across the river. Take a close look at the inn sign — a rose gaining sustenence in a pint beer mug!

Longworth: This is the birthplace of R.D. Blackmore, the novelist and author of Lorna Doone, and of Dr John Fell, who became a distinguished Dean of Christ Church, Oxford. Reputedly, he died of shock in 1649 upon hearing the news of Charles I's execution.

On one notable occasion Dr Fell threatened a particularly lively undergraduate at Christ Church with being sent down from the College. However, if the student would straightaway translate from the Latin Martial's epigram on Sabidius, Fell would allow him to stay. Literally the epigram is 'I do not love thee, Sabidius, nor can I say why. I can say only this, I do not love thee'. The exuberant student, with immense presence of mind, translated:

> 'I do not love thee, Dr Fell,
> The reason why, I cannot tell;
> But this I know, and know full well,
> I do not love thee Dr Fell.'

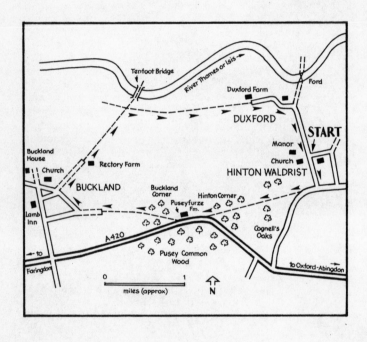

Hinton Waldrist
and Buckland

Introduction: This delightful all-season walk covers beautiful countryside offering extensive views over the Upper Thames and Vale of the White Horse. Starting at the small village of Hinton Waldrist, it passes through meadows by the River Thames, continues over and along the light sand soils of the limestone ridge and through the well preserved Estate Village of Buckland. Woodland and open countryside; hill and flat vale are all taken in during this easy and rewarding walk. If you have the time, take a particular look at Buckland House, Buckland Manor and Buckland Church — each in its own distinctive way offers a glimpse of this village's venerable history.

Distance: It is just under six miles in length and reasonably easy going. It took me about two hours to complete, but that was walking without a break, so add another half hour or so if you propose stopping along the route.

Refreshments: Hinton Waldrist has a shop but no inn. However, if you pass through Buckland at a suitable time you may decide to call at the Lamb Inn. Such is the nature of the countryside through which you pass, you may decide that a picnic is the best solution to the problem of refreshment.

How to get there: Hinton Waldrist is easily accessible from the A420 Oxford-Faringdon-Swindon road with three possible indicated turn-offs between Buckland and Kingston Bagpuize. Alternatively it is quite possible to start the walk half way through, in the village of Buckland.

The Walk: Start at the church in Hinton Waldrist and from there walk south through the village. When you reach the Longworth to Pusey road, turn right and walk out of the village. Some 500 yards from the junction, the road bears left. The footpath you need runs ahead over a field gate and through pastures running slightly downhill.

Cross two more gates in a couple of hundred yards and you will find yourself walking over undulating ground which slopes gently away to your right. You pass beside woodland to left and right; Great Pine Brake and Gognell's Oaks.

The path very soon plunges into deep oak woods at Hinton corner, and you may see several sets of beehives in these woods. The noise of traffic increases, and before you realise it, you have joined the A420 Faringdon to Oxford road.

Walk carefully alongside the road for 150 yards, passing the Georgian front of Puseyfurze Farm on the right. Immediately past the house, turn right, and in 30 yards bear left around the outside edge of a paddock. Open fields to the right give splendid views to Bampton and the distant Cotswolds. In a few yards you will fringe the hazel and oak woodland of Buckland corner on your left. In about 300 yards the path will cross open countryside to Buckland, which lies quite obviously on the skyline.

You enter the village through Summerside, and turning right at the first junction, follow the metalled road to the post office and stores at the village centre. Now is your chance to take a good look at the fine stone buildings in the village. University Hall is in Buckland House. There is also the manor house and a fine village church. See the Historical Notes.

At the post office bear right, and turn right by Court House in a few yards. You will soon walk downhill into open countryside with expansive views over the upper Thames valley to the range of Cumnor Hills on the skyline.

Follow the track to Rectory Farm, where you turn left over open fields, passing a solitary oak to your left, and in 500 yards encountering a hedgerow running to the right. Turn right following the hedge for about 500 yards. Having passed the grey-painted Ten Foot Bridge over the Thames to the left turn right in the corner of the field, along a trackway with a deep drainage ditch to the left.

In a hundred yards you pass a bridge and a little further on, take a narrow gateway to your left and pass over open pasture for some 400 yards, keeping the derelict buildings of Lower Newton Farm on your right. At the end of the pasture, another gateway and bridge leads into the next pasture. Follow the hedgerow ahead, which bears slightly left, pass under the pylons, and leaving the field by the corner gate, enter the rickyard of Duxford Farm.

You take the track in front of Duxford Farm, which has strutting peacocks on the front lawn. The track soon becomes a metalled road which you follow on a dog's leg route to Duxford.

I think the height of the thatched cottages at Duxford possibly had something to do with the proximity of the River Thames, here a few yards to the left. It is eminently floodable here, and the cottages have been erected on slight rises, attempting to keep themselves dry.

At Duxford, turn right. The road runs south and is level at first, but you will soon begin to walk sharply uphill and wind beneath the walls of Hinton Waldrist manor. You turn the corner and are back at the church, your starting point.

Historical Notes:

Hinton Waldrist: A thousand years ago, Hinton was a rectangular Roman earthwork called Achester, and the present oblong of village streets could well show the extent of that fort. A Motte and Bailey and certain traces of rampart can still be detected between Hinton Manor and Manor Farm.

The church was established by the Saxons, but essentially the present building dates only from the 13th century. Inside you will be able to see many marble tablets which make up an almost complete family tree of the Loder and Loder-Symonds's, for long connected with the manor here. Among them are John Loder (1781), Seymour and Mary Loder, Francis Loder (1724), Richard Loder (1836), John Loder-Symonds (1875), F.C. Loder-Symonds (1923) and Vice Admiral F.P. Loder-Symonds (1952).

The Manor belonged in early days to the St Valery family whose ancient castle stood near the site of today's manor guarding the river crossing at Duxford. It was from that time that Hinton gained its second name, for Waldrist is a corruption of Valery. But as the St Valery line became extinct the manor passed to the Earl of Winchester then the Earl of Northampton. It was later granted by Charles I at the ancient rent of £38 16s 8d to Sir Henry Marten. Somewhat ungraciously the manor passed to another Henry Marten, who signed Charles I's death warrant. In 1668 the house and lands became the Loders' property.

Duxford: This hamlet marks the ancient and regularly used Thames fording point over to Chimney, Aston and Witney. A pair of farms, three tall stone and thatched cottages, and a narrow lane threading between stately trees and colourful gardens, make up this hamlet. Its main claim to fame a couple of centuries ago was that, jointly with Hinton Waldrist, it held two fairs a year, visited not only by people from the White Horse Vale, but using the ford, by those from Oxfordshire as well.

Buckland: Sir John Throckmorton, at the turn of the eighteenth century, owned a fine flock of Southdowns. The 500 sheep were Buckland's and their Lord of the Manor's pride and joy. From them one day in 1811 at Newbury Sir John had woven a special coat. At 5 am the animals were shorn, the wool carded, spun and woven, and the entire operation took 13 hours and 20 minutes. Five thousand people watched the show and as a result, Sir John won a thousand guinea wager. For a century Newbury's record stood, but recently a similar task took as little as two hours in Australia.

Buckland Manor and House. It was about 1690 that the Throckmortons took over the Yate's manor, a 16th century stone house just north of the church. By about 1760 they had built a new mansion, Buckland House, designed by J Wood the younger, of Bath. The central block in mellow stonework is attached by vaulted passageways to two octagonal pavilions at opposite ends of the house, one formerly a chapel the other a Library. The large block behind the main house was added early this century by Romaine Walker and has, if anything, added to the house's charm and proportion. Unfortunately, it is not open to the public.

The church. It is impressive and well-proportioned containing Norman and Early English architecture in abundance. Take a look at the two rows of manorial box pews; the hatchment boards and brasses to the Yate family and Southby's of Carswell. Henry Southby (1797) was an early promoter and benefactor of Sunday Schools in Bath. He founded Buckland Sunday School giving an Estate at Thrupp near Faringdon to support it.

Faringdon and Folly Hill

Introduction: Faringdon is one of the most distinctive and yet untypical of Vale of the White Horse Market Towns. It has really much more in common with the limestone-and-wool background of the Cotswold towns, such as Fairford and Cirencester, than to the clay vale towns of Abingdon, Wantage or Wallingford.

Take, therefore a good look at the old-world Cotswold charm of Faringdon Market Place where this walk begins; at the fine stone buildings, the preponderance of substantial coaching inns, the distinctive and ancient church; Faringdon House, Faringdon Hill, and Faringdon Folly.

The route covers inviting countryside along the ridge of the Corallian Limestone, offering extensive views over the Vale of the White Horse to the south and the Upper Thames Valley to the north. It is for the most part open and undulating, and involves no steep uphill or downhill walking.

Distance: A short walk of two miles forms the basis of this circuit, but if you feel energetic, you can extend the walk into a five-mile circular series of footpaths leading through Littleworth and Wadley. Both routes are enjoyable and easy to follow.

Refreshments: In the Market Place are the Crown, Bell and Salutation. Faringdon Folly provides a fine site for a picnic. Sitting under the cool of the trees, the hill top offers an all-round panorama of surrounding countryside to entertain you. Bring a pair of binoculars if you can.

How to get there: Faringdon has easy access by road using

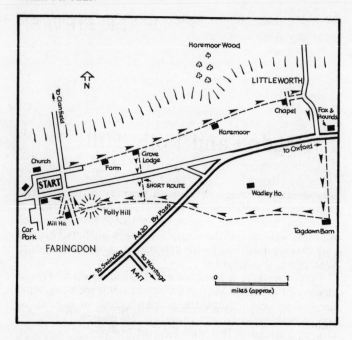

either the A420 from Swindon or Oxford or the A417 from Wantage or Lechlade. There is good car parking space in the Market Place and Church Street, with a further substantial car park behind the Bell Hotel.

The Walk: Before you leave the Market Place, by way of Church Street, take a particular look in the fine 13th century parish church, especially at memorials to the Pyes and Untons.

You walk gently uphill from the Crown; round the corner by the Salutation, pass the Radcot Road, and walk ahead for a few yards to the top of the street. The stone-covered bridleway runs ahead where the metalled road turns sharply right and runs gently uphill. Called Church path, this route was for Littleworth folk, who used the track to reach Faringdon before their village had its own church.

In about 400 yards you pass a farm, and the bridleway has

76

become a footpath passing along the top slope of a field, affording wide views to the left over the Upper Thames Valley. Keep the field boundary to your right and the downhill slope to the left. Some 600 yards further you come to a small cottage on the right, which is called Grove Lodge.

If you are taking the five mile circuit, continue now with the directions after this paragraph. For the two-mile walk, you now pass the cottage and turn right immediately after it. Keeping the hedgerow to the right, walk sharply uphill for about 300 yards to the A420, which you will then cross. The path continues opposite and slightly to the left, passing through a metal gate from the roadway. The track winds gently round to the right, and you keep Folly Hill on your right for a further 300 yards until you come to a signpost showing footpaths to both left and right. Turn right up the side of Folly Hill. You now join the five-mile circuit again and directions continue at the fourth paragraph from the end.

The five-mile walk carries straight on, past Grove Lodge, and you walk along the left hand of a pasture roughly parallel with the main Oxford road, which is away to the right.

You will see Haremoor Farm ahead, and the footpath passes to the left of the buildings. Haremoor Wood, a considerable expanse of oak wood, lies down to the left, lying in a slight valley running up the side of the limestone ridge.

On from Haremoor, the walk proceeds in the same direction, but the going may become harder and wetter underfoot as the path has been partly ploughed out. From the farm buildings keep the boundary fence to your right and aim for the metal gate a hundred yards over the field. You will now find youself in an arable field. Continue in the same general direction. On the skyline you will see two isolated trees: the path passes just to the right of them.

The village of Littleworth soon comes into view. Obvious on the edge of the settlement is a small and characteristic chapel. The path goes into the village just to the left of the chapel and crosses a stile on to a track. Turn right along this track, then quickly left. In a few yards is a metal gate through which you pass, then turn right on to the road and walk up the village street.

Some 500 yards further and you join the Oxford to Faringdon road. Turn left along the footpath beside the road. The Fox and Hounds lies ahead on the left. A few yards short of the inn a track turns right, off the road, which the walk follows, becoming a footpath in due course. As a footpath the walk follows a hedgerow to the left, and you will come to a prominent hedgerow ahead of you. Pass through this hedge and turn left, walk 40 yards, then turn right again. Continue across the field ahead to Tagdown Barn, which lies unmistakably some 400 yards ahead.

Turn right at the barn along a bridlepath which bears slightly to the left, then cross a ditch at the edge of Wadley Park. In a few yards the path takes a slight bend to the right, then continues on its previous line. In some 250 yards the path again bends slightly, this time to the left. At this point pass through a white gate on the right.

The footpath should cross the field diagonally, but in this case it is best to go round the boundary, keeping the crops to your right. At the next corner, by a small lake, turn right, making for the next white gate. Walk through it and bear half left across pasture. You are now back on the original line of the walk, and you shoul aim to keep the corner of Oxpen Copse to your left. At this point you pass through another farm gate. The footpath bears slightly left and here you walk ahead, keeping a fence and ditch to your left. The fence soon becomes a hedge and in about 600 yards, having crossed the Faringdon by-pass, you cross a bridlepath which runs round the base of Folly Hill. The indicated footpath is straight ahead.

You have now joined the two-mile walk and will find yourself ascending the side of Folly Hill through a tree nursery. From this point there are extensive views over the Vale to the Downs, a view described by Henry James Pye, Poet Laureate to George III, in his "Faringdon Hill." It contains a profusion of pastoral and woodland imagery, sometimes grotesque, such as

> Ye envious trees! Why does your leafy pride
> Stretched o'er the bending valley Wantage hide?

You will find that one footpath passes right over the hill beside the Folly on the right, built by Lord Berners in the 1930s. Another path encircles the summit of Folly Hill, with conveniently spaced seats from which to view the surrounding countryside.

Walk downhill from the Folly. The path very soon turns into a narrow lane running between high walls. In some 500 yards you come to the Stanford road, opposite Mill House, below which was the site of Faringdon's windmill, although the site is now regrettably hemmed in by modern housing.

Turn right along Stanford road on the raised footpath. At the junction with London Street, turn left to the Market, where the walk began.

Historical Notes:

Faringdon: The town had early royal and monastic links, for Saxon kings are believed to have lived here. Edward the Elder died at Faringdon in 925. A Castle built in 1144 was destroyed by King Stephen, while in 1205 King John gave Faringdon's manor to the Abbey of Beaulieu, which then built a small cell of that Abbey here.

Market House: This old Town Hall stands on pillars and has a largely open undercroft, which lets on to the market place down a series of steps.

Faringdon House: Once the seat of the Pye family, it lies north of the church. On the present site was an older building which was held for the King in the Civil War, and only surrendered in June 1646 on Charles' express orders after the fall of Oxford. Oddly, it was Sir Robert Pye, a Parliamentarian, who laid siege to his own house, and during the bombardment of the building from the lofty eminence of Faringdon Hill, the spire of the church was totally destroyed by cannon balls about 1645. The present building was erected by Henry Pye in 1780. He also became Poet Laureate in that year and later, Member of Parliament for the County of Berkshire. He wrote the lengthy poem called 'Faringdon Hill' reviewing the scenic beauty to be viewed from the summit. Pye sold the house in 1788, but Faringdon Clump was planted by his direction. The clump was a substantial grove of Scots Fir trees at the top of the hill, today sadly depleted.

Faringdon Folly: This tall, ornamental structure built at the summit of Faringdon Hill amid Pye's Fir trees, was erected in 1936 for the 14th Lord Berners to designs by the Duke of Wellington. It's intention was entirely as an observation tower, but has sadly been closed for most of the time since the end of the second world war.

The church: It contains much fine architecture and is rich in monuments and brasses. Take a look at the Pye and Unton chapels especially, and the fine tracery in the windows.

79

Wadley: The Unton family lived here between 1530 and 1650, and many of them are commemorated in the Unton Chapel at Faringdon, as are the Purefoys who gained Wadley Hall by marriage. Sir Henry Unton (1596) has a splendid alabaster altar-tomb. He was twice Ambassador to France and died in Paris but was brought to Faringdon for burial. He issued a notable challenge to Duke Henry of Guise, who spoke some slighting words about Queen Elizabeth, proposing a duel with 'such manner of arms as you shall like or choose, be it on horseback or on foot'.